Copyright © 1st edition 2018 Tanya Freedman

Published by Creative Hummingbird Results

All Rights Reserved. This book is a work of fiction. Names, characters, places, brands, media, and incidents are either products of the author's imagination or used fictitiously. Any resemblance to actual events, locales, or persons, living or dead, is entirely coincidental.

No part of this book may be reproduced, stored in a retrieval system, or transmitted in any form or by any means, electronic, mechanical, or otherwise, without expressed written permission in writing from the author.

Cover Vision by Tanya Freedman

Nobody's Baby But Mine/Gloria Silk

PRINT ISBN: 9780995197244

(LARGE PRINT ISBN: 9781989229026)

ABOUT THIS NOVEL

From USA Today Bestselling Author, Gloria Silk this is a gripping, romantic and sensuous novel of marriage, fidelity, fertility and the power of love.

"Gripping, romantic, sensuous and astute."

"New women's fiction that touches all of our emotions, fulfills our yearnings, and opens up new possibilities."

HOW FAR WOULD YOU GO TO PROVE YOUR LOVE?

5 Stars - TROUBLE IN PARADISE!!!
"Man, talk about losing a few inches around the waste. Yep, this tale has definite weight loss promise. If you're looking for a fast paced, easy to follow, smooth flowing read that captures your attention and holds it till the last word. Congratulations my friends you've found it. With all the twists and turns and surprises around every corner it keeps you on your toes. The characters and scenes were realistic and believable. I followed the characters along as their personalities transformed and blended. The detailed descriptions painted a vivid picture. The read seems to come alive right before your eyes. Remarkable job Gloria. Thanks for sharing." Kaye's Reviews, Goodreads.

THIS BOOK IS ALSO AVAILABLE IN LARGE PRINT FORMAT. PLEASE ASK YOUR LOCAL LIBRARY TO ORDER IT FOR YOU.

ISBN FOR LARGE PRINT: 9781989229026

NOBODY'S BABY BUT MINE
ONE SINGLE MOMENT CHANGES ALL THEIR LIVES

GLORIA SILK

REVIEW AND GET HOT RELEASE NEWS AND FREE EBOOKS

Want to receive (at the most biweekly) newsletters about Gloria Silk's news and free ARCs (advance reading copies)? I'd love to send you exclusive, exciting book news and special offers.

Please subscribe on Gloria Silk's Newsletter page now.

I also love to hear from my readers: **Email Gloria Silk now or after you've read this book. Your feedback is always appreciated as it helps me to constantly improve my craft and your entertainment.**

Do you review books because you love reading good quality fiction?

Then you're someone after my own heart!

As the best way of sharing great books with others is by far word of mouth and reviews, after you've read this book, please consider reviewing it.

I love receiving your emails telling me how much you enjoyed a certain book of mine, please keep them coming, and also it would help so much if you share your thoughts on any platform where you buy books, even if it's a quick one liner that shows you've read the book you're reviewing.

Remember, good books deserve to be shared with your friends and loved ones.

July, 2018: (Breaking the Chains renamed to) Healing Love - A young artist's craving for love endangers her business as well as her life. How can she turn her life around and find everlasting love?

FOR MORE ABOUT GLORIA SILK AND HER BOOKS, VISIT:
www.GloriaSilk.com.

ACKNOWLEDGMENTS

This novel has been in the making for over twenty-three years. Since the story line grabbed hold of my psyche and never let me go since the mid 1990's, I'm so happy to have finally done it justice. I'm proud of the novel which so many people helped me shape and layer over the many rewrites to its final production.

Among the many who have been invaluable are: Anna, Bethea, Kate, Michael, Natalia, Tara, Trenda, Yvonne…You've been incredibly generous with your time and expertise in all things editing, revising, cover design and all-round amazing support! Thank you, as always. You make my work and me appear even better than I had envisioned.

To Austin, my lovely patient husband who always says, "make something easy," whenever I ask what we should have for dinner. All the positive qualities of the novel's hero is based solely on your wonderfulness and unconditional love.

Is it really nearly three decades that we've been together?

Finally to my lovely readers who let me know how much my books entertain and help you. You're the reason I write and love waking up every single day to rush to my computer. Thanks from the bottom of my heart.

CHAPTER 1

MARCH

The March rain pelting the kitchen windows made Rachel think of tears. And there were indeed tears in her eyes as she told JT that their best friends' marriage was over. The inseparable love birds, Tina and Andy, were the last couple they thought would lose in the marriage roulette. Rachel had also thought that their two young children were another unbreakable bond.

Her husband frowned as he looked up from his poached salmon and asparagus laden plate. "I didn't even know they were having problems."

Her temples throbbed. She had been too self-absorbed with her own life and yearning for a baby that she hadn't noticed any signs or cracks in Tina's marriage.

Some friend you are, Rachel.

"He was having an affair with a friend of theirs since Justin was born. Tina didn't suspect a thing...It's so sad how everything can change so suddenly. Why would a man jeopardize his whole family life like that?"

How fragile life and relationships seemed.

Nervous for all marriages she thanked God for her own strong bond with JT. Despite their issues of unexplained infertility, their marriage was blessed even after seven-and-a-half years.

"I'm sorry to hear this. I'm shocked...but maybe he wasn't getting what he needed from her—"

"What? Tina's been a great wife and very patient with him all these years." She felt her anger rise thinking of Tina's meddling mother-in-law—so much like her own—and Andy's fledgling music production business, which had ostensibly kept him away from home for days at a time. "It's disgusting what he's done."

"I agree, but no one knows what really goes on behind closed doors." He sighed, "But there's never any excuse to screw up a marriage."

Rachel shook her head. "No, and especially with Emily and Justin...." How would Tina manage with her five-year-old daughter and almost three-year-old son on her own?

He shook his head. "He's a fool. I'm disappointed for them all." He glanced at her, his fork half way to his lips, "Don't worry, Rachel, I know how much you care for her. All you can do is be there for them." He then put a salmon morsel in his mouth.

"Communication is the most important thing in any marriage, right?"

She felt JT's eyes bore into hers as he watched her across the narrow mahogany kitchen table. Putting down his cutlery he reached for her hand nearest to him. She adored that sparkle in his gunmetal-grey eyes and that slow smile.

"We're not like the rest, to do anything stupid and ruin everything." With a quirked brow his thumb massaged the top of her hand.

Her heart skittered at JT's deep knowing expression the way it had when they met at a mutual friend's wedding in London nine-

and-a-half years ago. He seemed to always know how to brighten her moods, make her smile, feel safe and whole.

He kept her grounded, focussing on what mattered most; them: them, together.

Rachel would concentrate on her part-time job with Gareth Robinson-Brown's real estate agency and not drive herself crazy about why she was still not pregnant after five years of trying. She remembered JT's wise words after their last specialist appointment a couple of months ago to stay patient and positive and not let anyone stress her out. That was why she had given up running her own team in a Central London agency three years ago.

Neither did she get too involved in her younger sister's private life. Emotionally supporting the twenty-five year-old Abby without getting sucked into the turmoil of her sister's love life was proving wise and healthier for both sisters. She pushed aside the uneasiness she had felt seven months ago when she had met Rick, the new boyfriend. Abby had seemed happy with a bright 'I'm in love' smile at her trendy restaurant in Islington, but the phone calls had petered out over the last couple of months. Rachel resolved to call and see how she was doing.

In the meantime, she would be truly present for Tina. She took in a breath and slowly exhaled and felt a smile play on her lips. "I know you'd never dare stray, because I'd just have to kill you." She threw him an arch look.

JT grinned. "I'd never want to be with another woman but you, and you know it. And it can work both ways. I'd strangle any guy who even looks at you in that way." His eyes darkened, his passionate lips thinning into a resolute line on that handsome rugged face, making her smile broaden. "Like your old boyfriend we bumped into... where was that? The French restaurant soon after we met."

"Brandon." Her pulse raced for a few seconds and then settled. "It was our second date."

"Ah, so you still remember the name of that pretty-boy, no-good gigolo." The twinkling glint in his eyes was warm and inviting. "You'll have to make up for that, wench."

"I truly love you, JT. How did I get so lucky?"

He smiled again. "You're going in the right direction." He let go of her hand for the moment it took to push his chair back and come and stand beside her. Holding both her hands he raised her left one to his lips. His touch was always simultaneously calming and arousing. He leaned towards her. "Am I reading those sexy brown eyes right? There's more than one choice for dessert to make up for..."

She licked the corner of her lower lip while he stared at her mouth as if it was a luscious strawberry, his favourite fruit. Especially when served with melted semi-sweet dark chocolate.

"Devil's food cake and chocolate dipped strawberries."

His lips slowly gravitated towards her mouth.

Even after all these years together, Sundays were their full day and night for each other and no one else. Their routine became a variation of sharing a long shower or an indulgent hot soak in the tub before dinner.

Before long they lay in each other's arms against the soft cushions on the large Persian rug. The large fire in the regal fireplace shed heat and golden light over their naked skin and the plush cream throw. The intermittent crackling of the flames accompanied Nora Jones in the background. The light banter between them changed as JT gently placed Rachel's empty wine glass on the sofa table beside the plate with the single remaining chocolate-dipped strawberry.

He leaned closer. "I'll make you forget everything and everyone tonight." JT murmured low, nuzzling his lips against her ear and migrating to her other sensitive erogenous zones. Almost purring, she lay back welcoming his explorations. Her arms encompassed his broad shoulders. She closed her eyes and counted her lucky stars. Everything would work out, even filling the nursery with their gorgeous, healthy baby. Pushing the thought out by letting the languid feelings of their intimacy flood her mind, she gave herself over completely to the bliss.

"I'll always adore you." He groaned, inhaling into her throat. Her pulse and heart beats quickened as he explored her skin and his lips hovered so close to hers. "Don't ever doubt it."

"I know. I—I love you, too." Shivers of anticipation made her voice shake. Then they were kissing, hungry and sated at the same time. As always, his touch and sure kisses covering her tingling skin melted her insides.

Lightly, her shaking fingertips traced a butterfly-light line from his neck to his shoulders. His hard biceps stiffened at her caress. She loved his strong physique. Running impatient fingers through his thick silky hair she directed his head lower and kissed him deeper. She was home, warm and stimulated, marvelling how neither tired of making love with each other despite their pressures. His work and her constant hopes for a baby.

Almost of their own volition, her hands roved down his straining back muscles, as her legs tightened around his taut buttocks and hips to meld even closer into each other.

Everything outside their circle vanished. Well, almost everything.

CHAPTER 2

Rachel had to get out of the suddenly claustrophobic room in the house her boss was showing to a prospective client. Not only because yet again his pompousness was making her question why she continued working for him, but because she had to leave the cozy baby's room. It was decorated in warm yellows, greens and earthy browns. Biting the inner corner of her lower lip she envisioned the serene mother and her saintly Mona Lisa smile, with a new-born at her engorged breast, rocking gently in her feeding chair.

With every passing month she wondered if she ought to move to another part-time job instead of stoically taking Gareth's increasing irritability with life and business. He had been respectful and flexible three years ago when she had accepted this 'temporary' position of running his office a few hours a week.

"Gareth," Rachel cleared her throat and faced her boss who stood behind her by the bathroom entrance. "Why am I here for this showing? And can you just tell me who this prospective investor is?"

With their third child on the way the family living in this renovated, elegant Victorian in the outskirts of Oakwood were moving to a larger house. While Gareth Robinson-Brown was selling this house for them, he had already sold them their sprawling new home in Potters Bar.

"You'll find out soon enough. All you need to know is that his company already bought three properties in the past six months from the competing agents, and we'll do whatever it takes for him to switch to us." She had never heard him mention the name of the larger, more successful real estate agency up the Cockfosters high street, which he blamed for all his troubles. After making a show of looking at his watch, the bald man straightened his chequered cream and brown bow tie, smoothed the lapel of his black three-piece suit over his lanky form and left the room.

Fed up with his secretive behaviour, Rachel reminded herself that she was exactly where she had chosen to be.

You have a good life, with only one thing missing.

Inhaling deep but not-so-calming yoga breaths, she reminded herself she could leave her job any time she pleased thanks to JT's secure and well-paid Vice President position at Acorn Pharmaceuticals. She would continue working for Gareth at the local agency, until she was ready to quit to finally become a mother. Over three years ago, after Dr. Carter had suggested that stress could be a major factor as to why she wasn't getting pregnant, Rachel had given her one month's notice. Knowing her 'stay busy' personality, JT had agreed with her decision, believing she would be happier working locally part-time rather than staying at home.

Positive thoughts only.

Even now, on a cool, wet March Monday morning, Rachel enjoyed the waves of goose bumps remembering lying in JT's arms last night. She wasn't proud of how afterwards she had silently prayed, *let tonight be the night.*

After five years of trying to get pregnant, she was still living in hope. Surely many women even older than thirty-four got pregnant. JT always reassured her that one of these days their efforts would bear fruit, because they were so good together. Even while he had held her sobbing body after last month's unbearable disappointment, he had sounded so sure that she had let herself believe him. Again. The unexplained infertility with the complications of her long term painful endometriosis were obstacles they would overcome, and one way or another they would have their own child. Patience...

The doorbell interrupted Rachel's reverie. She sighed, this time holding on to the soothing calm of last night's sensuous and romantic memories. Easily conjuring up the scent of JT's fresh cologne as he had kissed her early this morning on his way out the door.

Following Gareth to the landing, she watched him rub his hands together as he pointed at the door below. "Do your job; let him in, woman."

She felt her boss behind her as she descended the stairs and opened the door.

Brandon Ross!

She heard her own gasp and her eyes widened.

The languid thoughts of a few moments ago dissipated and heat spread over her in the cool house. Staring at the tall frame of her old flame brought a flood of memories of their last time together. She had been twenty-four and he twenty-seven.

Her heart somersaulted as she smiled back at him.

"Won't you let Mr. Ross in, Rachel?" Gareth's voice had lost its acidity.

Standing aside, she blinked. She had hardly thought about him and only last night he had popped into her conversation with JT over their Sunday dinner. It was eerie to see Brandon here in the flesh after all these years.

She had forgotten how gorgeous and tall he was. How could he have hardly changed after ten years? He still wore his jet-black hair long, curling into his shirt collar under the open short Burberry coat. As he entered the hallway she couldn't help but watch those narrow hips and the thick thigh muscles under his tight designer trousers.

When he faced her, his eyes were clear emeralds with a hint of the secret depths of the ocean. Without him uttering a word, those vibrant eyes had always made her feel like she was the most beautiful woman, and no one else existed.

A tiny shock zapped through her arm as Brandon's hand swallowed hers.

Beside her she recognized the subtle edginess in Gareth's narrowed eyes. "I was surprised that you wanted Rachel to deal with you on this property. *I'm* the broker...." Gareth's voice quietened and shut off. Or had she just tuned him out?

Brandon's smiling eyes held hers. "Nice to see you again, Rachel Valentino." His deep baritone voice was still as delicious as bittersweet, dark chocolate. Feeling like a tongue-tied groupie she smiled back.

"And still as beautiful as ever."

For the first time in what seemed like years Rachel had the urge to giggle, but was keenly aware of Gareth's presence and underlying resentment. Her bubbling laughter would not be professional. Her earlier musings of the intimacy shared with her soul mate last night helped her find that Zen place within her. All was right with the world.

You've always achieved everything you've dreamed of, and your dreams of having JT's baby would also come true, and soon.

And that was all that mattered.

Until she looked up into Brandon's astute eyes.

CHAPTER 3

*B*randon smiled in that sexy way. "I've thought of you often."

Her throat suddenly parched, Rachel felt ravenous, although it was only ten-thirty in the morning. "Well, it's good to see you."

Trying to ignore his heated gaze, she was mortified to feel the sexual awareness between them reignite.

Gareth loudly cleared his throat, and Brandon released her hand. "I hope this was not a mere ruse to get to see your—"

"Not at all, Gareth." Brandon interrupted smoothly without breaking eye contact with her. "As we discussed, I'm well aware of Rachel's reputation and know that she'll be able to take care of all transactions I may make through your agency. And I am a serious investor, rest assured."

"But I'm not—"

Gareth interrupted her words with an eager nod and his benevolent businessman persona act. "Then I'll leave you two—"

"Thanks, Gareth." Brandon shook the man's hand, opened the door, smiled and waited for him to leave. Closing the door, Brandon turned to face her.

What had she looked like the last time they had met? She

wanted to see herself through his experienced eyes. She was glad her make-up and her favourite nearly nude lip gloss were freshly applied, and she wore her platinum hooped earrings, which added a touch of glamour to her stylish, honey-brown bob.

But despite any mutual attraction they were here to do business. She was married in the true sense of the word and its commitments. And, for all she knew, Brandon could be involved, too. "So, let me to show you around—"

He shook his head, smiling. "We've got plenty of time. Firstly, how have you managed to stay exactly the same after ten years?" The penetrating gaze warmed her insides. Her traitorous heart thumped louder within her chest.

She wondered if he chose not to see the tiny tell-tale miniscule lines around her eyes and mouth, the charmer. Brandon was only a couple of inches taller than JT's six-feet-two, but appeared much taller than she remembered.

Maybe I've shrunk. She reminded herself to stay real and on topic.

"You look great, too." She tried not to gush. "I—I see you're doing well on the property investments side, and taking advantage of the market, so let me—"

"Yes, it's a very good time to buy."

Rachel nodded, appreciating his business mind. He had known from his teens how to negotiate and go on his gut to buy low and sell just at the perfect time. While home owners shied away from moving, preferring to stay put, Brandon's family business had prospered by buying residential and commercial properties at those precise times. Of course, they had the luxury of sitting on them or leasing them to very particular overseas executives and other established clients.

As she led him through the high-ceilinged entranceway into the first large reception room she turned and asked, "What about your other silversmith business?" He also had a great artistic eye that had catapulted him to overnight success in his early twenties.

"Great, but these past few years I don't have as much hands-on time as I'd have liked."

"Ah, that's a shame. So, as you can see this is the spacious first reception room which—"

"Always straight to business," he chuckled and over her shoulder she saw him watching her instead of checking out the room. As she faced him, his warm, long, tapered fingers reached for her left hand. She tried not to react to the zinging sensation as he raised it and looked at the unmistakable wedding band and the glinting solitaire diamond of her engagement ring. She was proud of how imposing the one-and-a-half carat white diamond was, as if it represented the quality of her husband's love.

"Ah. I should have known."

Was that disappointment? Her heart swooped.

Almost shaking her head to clear it, she pulled her hand away. "Are you sure you're interested in buying more properties, because if you just wanted to meet me...."

"I'm interested." Interested in her or the property?

"Just so we're both clear, you plan to invest in more properties through GRB Agency, correct?" When he nodded she added, "I can only show you the properties, and you'll deal with Gareth with any offers. I no longer work on a commission basis." She gave him a professional smile and added, "So shall we?"

He held her gaze, shrugged and smiled in that familiar way. "Lead the way."

She nodded and her heels clicked purposefully up the hardwood stairs. So aware they were completely alone.

At the top of the stairs, standing outside the bathroom, he said, "After you've shown me around I'm sure you can spare some time for an old friend and prospective client, for a quick coffee." He looked absolutely certain what her answer would be.

Although he was hardly the type a woman could have as a platonic friend, her curiosity about his marital status or if he was with someone was piqued. Trying to calm her erratic heartbeat, her guilt lurched at the evocative memory of the last time they had still been an item. Their last night together, when she had rejected him. She knew she had hurt his pride. And he knew she was married.

Shrugging, she smiled, "Why not? Just for a short while."

"There's a quiet little café...."

Brandon held the bedroom door open for her.

CHAPTER 4

James saved the email he was composing as the tall, attractive redhead sat in the chair on the other side of his desk, and crossed her long legs with unpretentious grace.

He tried to dismiss his distractions and focus on the impromptu meeting project manager Lauren Mitchell had requested. In addition to the increasing pressure of the looming merger he also dreaded the impending family dinner this Friday. Work issues were merely doable challenges compared to the personal hurdles he faced with Rachel, especially where his family, namely his parents, were concerned. But nothing was insurmountable, he reminded himself.

Listening to Lauren making her very convincing case about why he should consider her for the new director position, he tried to remember if he had been this dogmatic and determined to advance his own career in his late twenties. Almost a decade younger than his thirty-eight years she was proving herself worthy to eventually become Vice President, Mac Tanner's successor. Knowing that she had been fast-tracked over the past two years on her career development program, he knew what she could accomplish with that drive. She carried herself with such poise and confidence and he admired her take-no-prisoners attitude.

"I agree with all that, Lauren, but Mac must have explained the predicament."

"Yes, but I suspect he failed to convince you of the qualities I possess that are perfect to fill this director position. I don't think there are any other worthy candidates."

They both knew she had one competitor.

"Dave Andrews has many more years of technical experience than you."

She took in a slight breath which forced her chest against her pale silk top under her dark blue skirt suit, and said, "But with due respect, I don't believe Dave has the same leadership focus that I have. You remember when I led a multidisciplinary team of PHD scientists to complete the AP307X project two months ahead of schedule? I believe in gathering the best team to get things done right the first time."

Diplomatically put, he thought, aware precisely of the project she was referring to, where Dave's way of dealing with a couple of his team members had nearly resulted in chaos in January. As VP, Mac Tanner had brought Lauren in and saved the day under James's supervision.

Lauren held his gaze with her large slanted hazel eyes. Watching her shimmering lips, he waited for her next words. "I spoke to Mac and he said it's up to you if I can go to Wellsley Valley with you both next month. Let me show you my skills and commitment. You won't regret it, Mr. Windsor."

"We've worked together for almost two years now, long enough for you to call me James, Lauren." He considered her offer and said, "The merger's going through smoothly, and I appreciate your conscientiousness, but we need you right here."

She continued to hold his gaze. "I don't feel that I'm being utilized to my full potential and I've not been as fulfilled in the work as I could be."

"I'm sorry to hear that."

She took in another breath; he sensed her effort to stay patient. "Full disclosure, another company has approached me with a similar Director position. But I believe I'd be a much better asset here, working for you. I'm committed to playing my part in the success of this company." Uncrossing her legs, she sat up in her chair and leaned slightly towards his desk. "I know I've only been here two years, but I can prove what I'm capable of, if you give me this chance at Wellsley Valley."

James had been in these situations too often to be surprised. Had he himself not played tactical Russian roulette in his earlier days of climbing up the corporate ladder?

Lauren's career appeared paramount to her. Like his wife's real estate agency had been to Rachel's when they had first met, up until three years ago. Even in that cutthroat, saturated business Rachel was never this forthright. When they had first met, maybe, but not these days...

The two women were as unlike as icing sugar and gunpowder. His beautiful, dimple-cheeked wife who couldn't wait to make them a family with their many babies, versus this subtly seductive important member of Mac's team.

He grasped his pen tighter. As Executive Vice President, one of his priorities was merging two important sites between London and Aberdeen, and restructuring the new organization, while also overseeing eight new product launches this quarter.

Lauren's credentials proved her strong technical expertise, even if she didn't have Dave's years of experience. She had proven her skills repeatedly, backing up her ambition with quick-witted intelligence, proving she was more than capable of handling the coveted but demanding Director role.

However, James also listened to his gut and something wasn't quite right. As a happily married man, he wasn't worried about working closely with Lauren. This director position, which brought Lauren here, was open solely because of his colleague's indiscretion with his personal assistant. The truth always reared its ugly head. It had cost Phil Blackmore his job, his reputation in the industry and his marriage.

His throat constricted and he laid down the pen before he broke it.

You're a professional and nothing like your weak-willed father. And if you promote Lauren it is because she warrants it and keeps proving herself more than capable.

He needed some more time. "Then the final decision is yours to make." He returned her unwavering stare. "But," he found himself adding, "Considering your many contributions which have already made positive impact on the company, I'll think about your request. I'll speak with Mac and Dave and get back to you by Thursday."

Doing his due diligence would reassure him it was his professionalism and not his ego making the final decision. Focussing on what was best for members of his staff and the company's long-term success was his job.

Lauren's face lit up with genuine pleasure as she stood up and offered her hand over the desk. Her hazel eyes sparkled—no, at this close vicinity he saw that they were hazel-green eyes. "Thank you, James."

He was taken aback for a moment at how she looked at him as if he were a powerful hero.

CHAPTER 5

In the crowded café sitting at the intimate bistro table with Brandon, the scent of roasted coffee beans and vanilla smelled extra sexy to Rachel.

Still exuding the same devil-may-care confidence with a polished sophistication, at thirty-six Brandon seemed more settled and calm in his success. His almost sculpted physique was perfectly trim. She averted her eyes for a moment. The gym had been her other rival alongside his business.

Was his unruly hair naturally this shiny, blue-black shade? Why did her husband seem so much older than him? Only two years his senior, JT believed that people took him more seriously in business since the dark metal-silver hair had pervaded his temples a couple of years ago.

She fidgeted in her seat when memories of those fun-filled months spent with Brandon heated her veins. His raw energy had ignited and stoked her sexually liberating side. She recognized his aftershave, with its tangy fresh, yet musky fragrance, so powerfully masculine. The scent of sin.

His easy smile still dazzled her. She shed her rain coat.

She sipped at her large cappuccino but no longer wanted her chocolate almond biscotti. "So, how's life been treating you?" She asked too enthusiastically.

As he recounted some of his business successes she remembered how driven he had been. Ambitious and a big dreamer, weeks into their relationship when she was disappointed that he wouldn't see her for over a week while away on a work trip, he had told her that his business would always be his number one priority.

She had taken his word for it, and realized that he wasn't the committing type. She had become certain after four months of dating that he would grow bored of her. Even at twenty-four she had known that she needed and deserved more than what Brandon was offering.

What about now? Was he married? Had he fallen in love again —if indeed he'd meant it when he'd admitted he loved her; did the words count when they were said in the heat of making love?

Why did it matter? She put down her cup a little too harshly.

She bit the inner flesh of her lip and paid attention to him. Now, with his wiser, calmer aura, Brandon's eyes didn't roam to all corners of the room.

"But that's enough about work—what about you? So, who's the lucky guy you married? Not George." Brandon's smiling eyes twinkled with curiosity.

"No. He was my friend. Still is. He's married and has a baby girl and another one on the way.... My husband's name is James Windsor. I call him JT." She had met him when she had least expected to be interested in romance or any man, after her deep feelings for Brandon.

"Did you meet him before or after you—we—broke up?"

"After, of course." Rachel tried to be patiently magnanimous.

Her frank expression must have convinced him. "How did you meet?"

"At a wedding." She answered.

"He was single?"

"Of course." She frowned. She shunned the thought of Abby who *had* unknowingly got involved with a married man. The sanctity of marriage was all-important to Rachel and JT. Brandon had, however, admitted years ago to his couple of "little affairs with unhappily married women."

She fidgeted in her seat again.

"Did it happen quickly, like you'd wanted?" he asked. When she nodded he said, "So he's the perfect Prince Charming." There was that smile again. "What does he do?"

"He's EVP in a large pharmaceutical company."

"Executive Vice President… Clever guy." He paused. "Is he the one I saw you with at that restaurant … a few months after…"

"Yes." Rachel felt the same heat in her face at the memory of the awkward tension between the men.

"Good looking guy. Nice catch." His jealousy was obvious.

"We happened to fall deeply in love." Her guilt resurfaced about rejecting Brandon.

"I thought you loved me… I'm sorry." He looked down into his half empty coffee cup. "I'm glad it's worked out for you. How long have you been married?" As if it didn't really matter.

"Eight years next month."

"And have either of you got the seven year itch?"

Her breath caught in her throat. "Of course not. I don't like—I have to go—" She shoved her arms into her coat sleeves and got her bag, and was about to stand up, swallowing down her disappointment.

What had she expected?

"This was a mistake. Gareth can show you more—"

"No, Rachel, I'm sorry. Really." He touched her hand and leaned closer. "I suppose seeing you again has brought all these feelings—" His admission kept her in her seat.

"I really thought we'd make it, you know?"

Her brows raised, her heart stopped beating for a moment, and then stumbled to catch up with the erratic rhythm. Guilt intermingled with flattery. "But you were still so young, establishing your business and..." Rachel sighed. "I'm sorry, but I really believed it was no use staying together if we were after different things. It was the best thing for both our sakes."

"Do you still believe that?"

For a split moment she thought of JT's aloofness sometimes when work pressure took over. "Of course, I love my husband very much."

"But we can still be friends. You can never have enough good friends. Right?"

Over my dead body, or marriage at least! You're not the kind of guy I can imagine having as a friend. She smiled, trying to push aside the heat he evoked within her. Her college mate George who had helped her pick up the pieces after she'd broken up with Brandon was a friend. But she had never had the hots for him. A smile played on her lips imagining JT's face if she introduced Brandon as her old 'friend'. From their past exchange, there would be a duel or at least a cerebral brawl for the flattered damsel's honour.

Common sense prevailed, even if Brandon was in a committed relationship. "Let's just keep it all professional, Brandon."

After a moment he asked, "So do you have any children?"

"No, not yet." Did he remember how much she had always wanted kids? "We're trying."

She would have loved to have at least two children to talk about, to make her marriage sound perfect and further cemented with unshakeable love.

Through tears prickling her eyes, she saw the sympathy in Brandon's eyes. It was unbearable.

"I understand." Then he started discussing his company and the family's business diversifications. "I'd like to make an offer on the house we just saw, and also you can put together a list of all available properties that are near or around the shopping centers and tube stations." He then gave her a number of how much money he was willing to spend over the next year or so with GRB Agency.

Rachel was flabbergasted at the huge sum, but listened to his further requirements and plans. Gareth *would* be pleased.

CHAPTER 6

She noted that he wore no wedding ring but he was not the type to show shackles of belonging to another human being, even in the name of love.

He must have caught her look. "I'm not married." He smiled openly. "Never been."

Egocentric hope made her blush as he studied her. Was he still... *Don't be ridiculous*. He was merely not the marrying type.

"Are you...involved?" As he shook his head again, she said, "Impossible to believe you haven't been snared by a determined woman who wouldn't take 'no' for an answer." Her voice didn't sound as nonchalant as she had hoped.

"Thanks, but obviously I'm not as irresistible as you think —thought."

"Maybe you've just been too busy."

"No. The right woman didn't..."

She held her breath feeling warm all over.

"... Materialize, I suppose. I've screwed things up..." He touched her hand.

Was she the one who got away?

"Don't look so worried." His fingers on her hand sent currents of dangerous sensations into the rest of her. "I've been around, but I seem to have the knack of falling in love with too spirited women. Maybe I'm just too possessive." He lowered his eyes for a moment.

"You, too possessive?" In those sex-crazed months she had taken for granted he was incapable of expressing himself in any other way than sexually. She would have opened up to him even more...

He added, "I thought *we* were good together. I thought I'd shown you that I loved you."

Once more Rachel's heart jumped painfully at his frankness. A far cry from the younger Brandon. Had he always cared for her more than he'd let on? Had he matured and become more sensitive? A decade was a long time.

Yes, remember in whose arms you belong. Last night Brandon had been miles from her mind, but sitting here... "Brandon, I—I..." It sounded like a whisper.

His astute gaze made her thirsty, hungry. The stifling raincoat added to the languid ache melting inside her. Her armpits tingled.

"Rachel," he said it as softly, his hand continuing holding hers on the bistro table, apparently as ignorant of the crowd and noise around them.

At a sharp sound of breaking crockery, she blinked. What if someone recognized her, drinking cappuccinos with another man, staring into each other's eyes?

Enough reliving your twenties and 'what-ifs.'

"This *was* a mistake, Brandon."

As if the snake charmer had stopped playing the flute, her own words shook her out of a trance. She had to escape. Slinging the strap of her bag over her shoulder with shaking fingers, she got up. Her forced smile wouldn't oblige. Her chair screeched loudly against the tile floors echoing in the suddenly confining space.

With unsteady fingers, she brought out her mobile phone and stared at the time. "It's been... nice to see you, to catch up and everything." She was more in control while standing over him by the tiny table. "I'll organize the papers for you to sign. They'll be ready for you at the office tomorrow morning."

"I'll pick up the papers and we can discuss the properties over lunch."

"Sorry, no. It'll be better all around if you deal with Gareth. And if you don't want to, then that's up to you."

Frowning again, Brandon stood too. "I want to work with *you* directly. I'll behave." He stood up easily and held her hand between his two. He sighed, "I suppose seeing you again has brought back memories.... I promise I won't bring up the past and make you uncomfortable. Now will you agree to be my direct liaison?" That playful Elvis smile took the edge off the threat.

She was old enough to see that he was biding his time for more. She shook her head. "No, it's too late for that. I'm sorry."

"Okay, not even as friends but purely working relationship—?"

Was her uneven breathing betraying her? "We both know that won't work. I'm a happily married woman. And I'm not one of those women who need you to make them feel good or better about themselves."

Brandon's eyes widened, "You've never been just another woman to me, Rachel."

The frankness was too much for her. "Stop. I have to go." Her heart constricted at his disappointed expression.

He let go of her hand, pulled out a small silver coloured card and gave it to her. "It's got my mobile phone number on it. Call me, any time." His intense look tempted her to wallow in his aura, to see herself through his eyes; young and attractive, feeling wanted by such an Adonis with green eyes.

Brandon leaned closer to her and his evocative aftershave filled her senses again. He raised her warm hand to his sensuous mouth. Her body reacted as if he'd kissed her more intimately.

Shaken, trying not to sigh aloud, Rachel said, "Goodbye."

Turning away, she pocketed his card in her voluminous bag and wondered if she would ever use it. *Of course not, silly.*

Her heels beating out a staccato rhythm against the tile floors she brushed through the new throng of coffee drinkers at the entrance. All the while feeling Brandon's eyes on her.

Outside, taking in a deep refreshing breath of the spring breeze, her mind reeled. After not breathing properly for too long, deep yoga breaths hurt her lungs, but didn't help lighten the heaviness within her ribcage.

Would she tell JT about having had coffee with an old-flame? Why bother? Despite Brandon's words fuelling her latent fantasies, she wasn't like her mother. Not only did she take her marital vows seriously, she was also committed to JT to infinity. She would tear up Brandon's business card as soon as got back to her desk.

Gareth would have to deal with Brandon, and that was it.

She tried to calm herself after the revitalizing feeling Brandon had reawakened. How happy she had been in the past hour. Her obsession with having a baby had fled—she hadn't thought about babies at all—and how good that had been!—until Brandon had asked about the one failure in her life.

Now crazy questions popped into her mind. What if... What if she had waited and married Brandon... would she have been a mother already?

Or...

What if Brandon could get her pregnant?

Yep! You've finally lost your mind! Get a bloody grip!

CHAPTER 7

Sitting in the large dining room of his childhood home in London, James felt rather than saw his mother's excitement. He glanced at her as he sliced at his roast chicken breast on his plate and right on cue she said, "We have some great news." Grace, his elegant mother with her fine blonde hair in its austere bun at the nape of her neck, held her small hand against her delicate looking collarbone and upper chest. "Danielle is expecting another baby."

Someone's cutlery clanged against a plate and Rachel nearly jumped beside him. He looked down and realized his heavy silver knife had chipped the edge of the Royal Doulton dinner plate in front of him. The pale blue of the rose pattern now looked as fractured as his equilibrium. He didn't need to look at Rachel to know how she felt inside. He had the same coiling pain writhing within his gut.

Ignoring his mother's frown when she saw the damaged plate he looked across the table at his younger brother and at Danielle sitting next to Adam. "Congratulations, Adam, Danielle. That's wonderful." He loved his adorable, cute nephews, and even as a private person who kept a picture of Rachel in his wallet, on his busy desk at work he enjoyed their great baby photo of when they were four months old.

But this hurt on some level, especially for Rachel.

"She just told me this morning but I couldn't wait until dessert to share the news. The twins will be almost three years old by the time September comes round," Mum chatted away. "And I'll help as much as I can, of course."

James felt his mother's eyes on him and then on Rachel. "Don't worry, even when—or I should say if —you two get going and give us another grandchild, I'll make sure to get the perfect nanny for you. I can't be expected to drive all the way to your neck of the woods, now can I?" She shook her head and picked up her crystal water glass, still studying him and Rachel.

He watched Mum raise it to her thin lips and say, "Unless you've changed your minds and are rethinking about moving back here? It would be easier to get to your work from here."

He shook his head, "No, Mother, we're happy where we are, and you don't need to worry about any of that. *When* we're pregnant you'll be one of the first people to know and we'll take care of the all the practicalities."

"Well, suit yourselves, but—"

"So how is that business deal going, Adam?" James knew Mum didn't like him interrupting, but he could either change the conversation or lose it altogether. He could shout, *It's not only Rachel's suffering because of her debilitating endometriosis that we're not pregnant yet, it's my low sperm count too, but because she's such a loving and big-hearted woman she's keeping my secret.*

It hurt him how despite his repeated explanations in private, his mother ignored Rachel's agonizing heavy periods and cramps, and how she dismissed that she was committed to her local job in Oakwood. But what was the use of talking about anything real or deep? Better to discuss the weather and business—because even politics or any family news invariably became hot beds of smouldering arguments or gossip.

As the still blushing Danielle asked Rachel about a savoury cheesecake recipe, Adam looked relieved to share the latest about his property development project in Manchester. Only half listening, James spied Rachel's hands gripped on her lap. Slowly while nodding, his fingers gently covered her left fist and he felt it relax somewhat.

William, his silent father, sat at the other end of the dining table nursing a much refilled tall glass of red wine. As always, he seemed to be in his own world.

He couldn't remember ever having any meaningful conversations with him. In his mid-fifties when he had owned an ink and spray-paint manufacturing company, Dad had broken his marital vows with his partner's secretary, the mousy widow in her early forties. Then, inevitably, the truth of his three-year affair had come to light. Even now, his blood curdled at his mother's acceptance, or rather complete denial, of the 'indiscretion'. The twenty-one-year-old James had lost respect for her for giving Dad a second chance.

After moving out, he'd never looked deeper into his parents' relationship.

Years later, after meeting and falling in love with Rachel, her empathy to his feelings had helped him heal and grow. After the way she had been forced to mature with her own difficult childhood and into her twenties her courage and positive outlook on life made him grateful for the opportunities his parents had given him.

Now the retired William spent many of his days golfing and playing poker every Wednesday night with his three remaining buddies. Grace kept herself busy with the house and grandchildren and seemed content enough with her lot. In their late seventies, his parents didn't strike him to be that old but they had already lost a few friends to heart-attacks and to cancer.

All that mattered to James was that they were healthy and had everything they needed. Now at thirty-eight, he had his own wife and future family to nurture. From Rachel's warmth and the way she completely accepted him and his flaws made him certain she would never be unfaithful to him. He also knew that *if* he ever strayed there would be no second chances with her. And he wouldn't blame her.

Take a leaf from your ever-patient wife despite what she's going through. He admired her constant hopeful disposition in all aspects of their life together despite their current obstacles.

However, in the past week something about her was different.

Standing up, Rachel excused herself. Her shoulders rising, her face pale, she almost ran towards the bathroom.

"Yes, squash this Saturday works." He stood, too. "Sorry, Adam, let me check on her."

He heard his not-so-subtle mother's whisper as he strode out of the dining room, "I can only hope and pray that Rachel's finally having pregnancy sickness."

Gritting his teeth he heard Adam say, "Mum, for God's sake, don't be so crass. It's unfair. They're going through so much, don't add to it."

James gripped the door handle of the powder room at the end of the long corridor, "Are you okay, Rachel?"

At her gasp and groan he knew what was wrong. "Let me in, please." He said gently and heard the latch click.

Rachel was leaning over the sink holding her stomach, tears on her flame-red cheeks. "No, JT, I can't bear this anymore. I just got my period, right now, this moment. Can you believe it? And I'd hoped that this time... It was delayed for almost ten days!" He heard her deep intake of another breath, as if she was trying to stay sane. "What if I *was* pregnant? I refused to take a test... but, oh, God, JT. I don't know what to do. I'm getting so desperate that..." She hiccupped.

Sod this! He pulled her into his arms and held her tightly. He felt her agony as she tried to contain her emotions.

"Take another slow breath, darling." He massaged her upper

back, kissing the side of her warm temple. "We'll get there, together. I—I'm happy for Adam and Danielle, but it's hard for me, too, to hear about...their news. But we're strong, together." He said softly and as minutes passed, her tension abated somewhat and her breathing seemed to come a little easier. He pulled his head away far enough to look into her haunted, pain-filled eyes.

"I want—we have to see Dr. Carter. Please." She whimpered. "I'd rather do the tests than let more years go by, just waiting and praying and going crazy."

"I wish there was more that I could do, maybe my sperm count—"

She shook her head, her wet eyes scanning his face, "No, that's not the problem, the doctor confirmed the last time. It's me, trust me."

He saw how the endometriosis was causing her more agony, and wished he could grant her their one and only wish. And he would do anything for her.

He nodded, accepting what they were both committing to. She wanted to get the more invasive exploratory tests to see if IVF was an option. "Okay, darling." He studied her face, "We'll do this together, but I can't keep watching you suffering like this, it tears me apart. And neither will I let you risk your life trying to get pregnant. You understand that, right? Nothing is more important to me than you."

Fresh tears welled up in her eyes as she nodded.

"Let's go home." He sighed deeply as she hugged him back. And despite the relief in her beautiful brown eyes, he felt tension rise in her rigid body.

He was happy for Adam and his growing family, but it would have made his life a little easier if his mother tried to be more sensitive towards what Rachel was going through. But he knew who he was dealing with. Somehow, along with the growing pressure at work, he would make sure he was there with Rachel every step of the way.

CHAPTER 8

"I've talked with Dave," James told Mac the following Monday. "He says he's content to stay where he is. For now. Especially with the personal stuff he's going through." The poor guy was going through a terrible divorce. Weren't all divorces terrible?

The burly, balding VP scratched his short greying beard and nodded. "I know. He said he'd prefer not to relocate to the wet and gloomy Wellsley Valley. Don't blame him. But…" Mac studied him. "I'm still concerned about the politics of promoting Lauren over him."

"I understand. Lauren may be young but her fresh outlook is exactly what Acorn needs at this phase of the merger. Her commitment to the betterment of the company is inspiring." He then added, "If Dave starts making waves let me know."

"She's impressed you." Mac smiled, and then shrugged. "She usually delivers on time, no matter what or who's involved. And her staff respect her."

James could have called her bluff when she had threatened to jump ship, but he could not afford to lose high-calibre staff. Elevating Acorn to the top three niche Pharmaceutical companies in Europe took dedicated and committed employees. Like Lauren Mitchell.

The takeover was a tough challenge all around, and Wellsley Valley came with three hundred and fifty set-in-their-ways employees waiting to fight any change and new Acorn Pharmaceuticals changes.

"Regarding her current position," James said. "You believe Katherine Lee is ready to fill in until we get the right replacement?"

"Yes, and Lauren seems confident in her."

James nodded as he noticed Lauren sashaying her way towards his door. Mac stood up. The smiling redhead entered the office and shook both his and Mac's hands.

After congratulating her Mac left.

James warned her, "You know it won't be easy at Wellsley Valley. They've done things a certain way for sixty years and we'll come up against a lot of opposition with our new ideas and higher output expectations."

"I love a challenge, James." Her eyes shone and he tried not to read anything in them.

"And what about the almost all-male workforce?"

"I can handle chauvinism, if I may be blunt."

Considering her words, he nodded. "Good."

"Thank you for this opportunity. You won't regret it. I'll do my best to prove your faith in me isn't misplaced."

That barely veiled hero-worship twinkled in her eyes. He missed that expression on his wife's face.

~

On Wednesday mid-morning, after another long meeting outside the large conference room, James saw the smiling Lauren slide through the grumble of crowds towards him. "That was a very dynamic presentation, James. Makes me proud to be working for you." She seemed excited, primed for higher things. He tried not to make it obvious when appreciating her tight tan suede skirt and white shirt that showed just enough... femininity.

"Are you available for a drink before the two o'clock meeting?"

He paused only for a moment. "I don't think that's necessary. But thanks."

He saw surprise in her eyes and then she burst out laughing, bringing attention from their colleagues. "I'm sorry, I didn't mean...I don't make it a habit of asking men I work for..." She shook her head, amusement still shining in her catlike hazel-green eyes.

"A few of us are getting together at the Mowbray for a celebration drink."

Ice-cold realization nearly drowned him and his ego. "Yes, of course. Good idea." He cleared his parched throat.

Towards lunchtime, tempted not to go, he decided to make a quick appearance. To keep up the morale, be one of the boys.

Striding towards the Old Mowbray at High Holborn, he ignored the passers-by, anaesthetised to the noise and putrid traffic fumes.

Entering the laughter filled, dimly lit pub, James recognized many Acorn employees drinking their pints and wine by the bar, dispersed within the right corner of the pub. Lauren had a colony of the company bees buzzing around her. The glossy scarlet lips turned up at the corners at the sight of him, as if enjoying a private joke.

Lauren pointed at the empty stool beside her at the bar and he pushed his way towards her. "I took the liberty of getting you a pint." What was her tall, dark glass laced with and how many had she had for her to look at him like that?

He thanked her, picking up the frothy pint. Someone hit him on the back and he almost choked on his first gulp. It was Jeff from Analytical Development, his half-hidden smirk under the wispy ginger moustache as irritating as ever.

James focused on Jeff as Lauren vacated her seat and weaved her way to join others a few feet away.

"Good luck to you, old boy." Jeff said, his eyes staring after Lauren.

"With what?"

"The Wellsley Valley trip."

"It'll be fine. Our Scottish friends will just have to learn a new way of doing things—with twenty-first century technology. Acorn style."

"I meant going with Lauren Mitchell."

"Mac will be there too. What's your point? She's very capable."

"And very young and ambitious."

"Yes, she is. Isn't that what we need; loyal people who'll work hard for the company?"

Jeff continued eyeing Lauren, his moustache twitching slightly on his fleshy face, his double chin pink from the strain of being kept inside the too small collar. For a split second James fantasized about hitting the middle-aged guy in the jaw. The way married men acted like over-sexed teenagers, drooling with lecherous innuendoes and stories of mostly untrue conquests, turned his stomach. Driven by ego or mid-life crisis.

Shuddering, he imagined the old boys betting "fifty quid to see how long James lasts out of the bombshell's clutches."

Was he at the receiving end, or was he being paranoid?

CHAPTER 9

He put the waves of nausea down to lack of lunch, too quick mouthfuls of his lager, and the noisy crowds he never enjoyed.

He listened and evaded Jeff's further veiled questions intermingled with inconsequential small talk. He checked his thoughts to ensure not to give away confidential information. Redundancies would affect the spectrum of the company, nationwide, and everyone was on edge.

Noticing Katherine nearby, he took his excuse to escape Jeff. Talking with the petite woman with black straight hair and shy eyes about her interim position of stepping into Lauren's shoes, James was glad to hear her talk so confidently about the opportunity.

From afar he saw Lauren using her hands in smooth strokes like a composer controlling a favourite piece of hypnotic music. She pushed her auburn hair back over her slender shoulders. Charm oozed out of her every movement. He imagined her honeyed voice weaving a hypnotic spell over her receptive audience.

A few feet away he noticed Graham, Director of Legacy

Product Management. His acne-scarred face burned puce red, making James suspect he was too stressed for his own good. He made a mental note to have a longer informal chat with him to put his fears at rest; that his job was secure and his family income assured, at least for the foreseeable future.

But right now he ought to be at his desk, fully immersed in the current project's complexities. About to turn to put down his nearly empty beer glass, he came face-to-face with Lauren.

He stood straight and heard her say, "I hear you live in Oakwood." Lauren's silky voice heated his right ear as she stood too close to him. The party she had held captive a few seconds earlier had dispersed.

"Yes."

"So do I. I'm on Trent Drive." It was unwelcome news, as if she had engineered that. She was saying something about cars and emergencies.

How would Rachel see Lauren? What an absurd thought. Rachel was all love and warmth, while Lauren was career driven above all else. One was a survivor, one the prey. Fire and ice. Rachel never used her feminine wiles.

When Lauren seemed to wait for a response he tried to smile away his embarrassment. "I'm sorry, I didn't hear you. It's a bit too loud here for me."

This time he concentrated on her words.

"My car's in for service, may I impose and get a ride back tonight?"

He gulped and agreed after a beat or two. Slowly he nodded.

"You leave the car at Oakwood station, don't you?"

Again he nodded, breaking eye contact. "Yes. No trouble."

He resisted the urge to loosen his tie and collar when Lauren's mischievous eyes darted to his left hand holding the beer glass. He relinquished it on the nearest table beside them, which gave him the opportunity to look away from her for a moment.

A hollow beat drummed in his temples at the prospect of travelling and working closely together with Lauren—and Mac, of course—at Wellsley Valley next week.

James averted his gaze.

In the pit of his stomach, something balled into a tight fist.

~

"Hi Lauren, it's Marilyn." Lauren's back stiffened in mid-turn to the fridge. She nearly dropped the eggs at hearing her step-mother's voice after all these years. Almost half her lifetime ago, she had told her father and Marilyn that she needed no one.

"It's your father's sixtieth birthday next month, as you know. And I thought you'd like to come to a party I'm organizing. We'd all be delighted to see you. I'll email you the invitation and all the details, but in the meantime you may call at home or on my mobile. The number is—" Lauren deleted the message. Although she had all the numbers in her own mobile she would never use them.

Fleetingly she wondered if her father knew his wife had invited his estranged daughter. Maybe he'd take one look at her and wonder if Lauren planned to ruin his celebration. She had a good mind to do just that, but she was no longer a wounded fourteen-year-old who hated everyone around her.

She ground her teeth at the familiar bitter taste of the injustice she and her mother had suffered. She shoved the memories of her past to the dark corners of her mind. But from her instant headache and clenched chest muscles the emotional betrayal was still obviously alive and raring to seep back into her present.

She wasn't proud of the last time she had seen her father and his other family in the lavishly decorated dining room of his new house. But what had they expected from a fourteen-year-old? She had accused her well-meaning step-mother and father of being ignorant, and that she would never ever live with them and watch them spoil her three-and-a-half-year-old half-brothers. She had shouted at them, "Not in a million years! I'm no charity case. I despise you and I'd rather live with Uncle Murray." She had hated her overbearing maternal uncle's family even more.

She had stood and glared at her frowning father with his reddening face, sitting with fisted hands in front of him at the head of the table.

Marilyn and the twins had stared at them. Lauren remembered wondering if Ethan was about to cry while Evan observed them all gripping his airplane baby spoon in his little hand.

At that time it hadn't mattered if they were nice and sweet, with their little ginger heads and hazel eyes so much like her own, Lauren saw nothing but the injustice.

She wouldn't contact her step-mother. They didn't need her and she needed no one. Her plans were going in the right direction but she wasn't ready to face her father just yet.

CHAPTER 10

It was almost midnight when Mark and Annabel left and Rachel was still in the kitchen clearing up. James did not like her sombre silence. Yet again, he wished she had cancelled or delayed their dinner when she'd realized she had ovulated. She probably hadn't wanted to inconvenience their friends with their baby sitters all pre-arranged. But when he heard that Annabel was pregnant he saw the writing on the wall of how the evening would play out. Although Rachel hadn't touched any drink, her movements became increasingly erratic as the evening drew to a close.

"Let's finish the rest tomorrow," he said gently. "Let's go to bed."

"I'm nearly finished."

"Don't let the evening get to you, Rachel. You promised. I know it's difficult to hear that Annabel's expecting their second...but at least you ovulated. Right? So let's go up." He soothed.

Still no response as she continued feeding the remaining cutlery in the dishwasher.

"I'll wait up in bed." James was turning away from her when

the plate in Rachel's hand crashed against the open dishwasher door.

She whimpered. His beautiful tortured wife in that slinky black dress which showed her sexy trim figure and long legs. As the dinner party had progressed, she was unable to keep her face from subtly betraying her inner emotions.

Automatically James held her rigid body. "It's all right, darling. Let's just go upstairs now."

She was predictable in her unpredictability. He sighed.

"Why's God doing this? Annabel gets pregnant so easily." Rachel looked and sounded like a helpless child as she pulled out two tissues from the box on the counter.

"At least you ovulated." He reminded her again, massaging her tense back.

"I ovulate two out of three months, and it doesn't help at all." She snapped. "And what if IVF tests won't work?"

His arms fell away from her. "I don't know, Rachel, but feeling sorry for yourself doesn't help either." His voice rose slightly. Well, damn it, he was tired. "Don't you think it bugs me too, the way Mark makes crude remarks about his virility?"

Rachel stopped sniffing staring up at him with wet, pink lids, the mascara smudged around her brown eyes.

"I told you to cancel it."

"I know what you told me." She pulled away from him. "Some women seem to know exactly how to get what they want. One minute they're having marital problems, the next she's pregnant despite what he wants." She lowered her eyes, as if conscious of how jealous she sounded. "Annabel intended to go back to work, and instead she gets pregnant again! And she doesn't even go back part-time, like I am."

"You're not doing it for the money. You know you can quit any time." Suddenly James wasn't in the mood to try to console her, never mind consider making love.

"I know." She cried even more bitterly. "All I want is one child."

He sighed. "I don't know why we call them our friends. We don't even enjoy their company any more. All they do is leave us like this."

"But I didn't think I'd react so strongly. You're so engrossed with work that sometimes I wonder if you still care as much as I do about having a baby. You're just so damned patient."

He took in a deep calming breath, but it wouldn't help.

~

As JT's hand fell away from her, Rachel looked up at him knowing what a mess she must have looked. JT's eyes darkened with anger, or was it disappointment?

Cold shock spread over her at the alien rejection as he withdrew his soothing touch.

"I don't know how much more of this I can take." He jabbed a finger as his chest. "Half the time I don't think you're listening to me. Lately all I get is how *you* don't have what *you* want. I want a baby too. How can you even question that?"

She watched him, hardly breathing.

"What about the things we do have? You take it all for granted. Don't deny it." He strode to the kitchen doorway as if not trusting himself to be near her. His tall muscle-bound frame dwarfed the big doorway.

"You're *not* supposed to be so stressed. I'm taking care of everything I can. I'm supporting you in whichever way I possibly can, aren't I?" He didn't wait for her answer. "And just because you've had such a rotten childhood doesn't give you the right to be insensitive to my feelings."

"I'm sorry, I didn't mean—" Rachel's tongue seemed stuck to the roof of her mouth. Her sadness and pain of a few minutes ago curdled into something more ominous.

"We both have to be patient." JT's face was flushed. "We have to wait. And with the pressure at work right now, the last thing I wanted was to entertain on a Friday after a busy week, but I tried for your sake. And frankly I don't feel like making love now."

"I've never seen you like this before, JT—" His frown stopped her words. She stared at him like he was an old abstract painting she had owned forever and was suddenly seeing the deeper message right there, where it had always been.

"I'm sick and tired of being the saint. Who'll listen to *me* for a change?" He poked a forefinger at his chest again. "Don't my feelings count for anything anymore? I'm more than just your personal sperm bank."

As he stormed out, she stood open-mouthed. Her heart constricting, her body felt as if it had shattered into a thousand pieces alongside the broken plate on the dishwasher door and kitchen floor.

She would give him a few minutes to cool off. Too self-absorbed, she hadn't seen this from his point of view and neither had she realized how Mark affected JT.

But quiet waters ran deep.

What the hell had she done?

She cleared up the remnants of the plate with shaking fingers, turned out all the lights and holding on to the polished banister, slowly mounted the stairs in the eerie silence.

The bedroom was dark with only a sliver of dim light from the bathroom shining in her path.

After finishing in the bathroom, Rachel crept into bed. Her heart still hammering in alien fear she held his rigid back and whispered, "I'm sorry, JT. I've been so self absorbed…"

Silence. JT's familiar deep breathing confirmed that he was asleep.

Filled with new emptiness, she realized that it was also the first time they wouldn't make love at the most fertile time.

But how could she blame him? He was right, she *was* obsessed. She was miserable with who she was becoming with every month —every day—of not getting pregnant.

How could she have stooped so low—and have become so desperate to even consider for a split second if her ex-lover could get her pregnant? Wasn't it JT's baby that she wanted to nurture and love?

And now she'd pushed her ever-patient husband too far.

Silent tears wet her pillow, as she hugged herself closer to the exhausted JT. The only man in the world who truly got her. God, she loved him.

CHAPTER 11

The next morning James awoke with a languorous sense of wellbeing. He shoved away the guilt about his silent, angelic Rachel curled up in her troubled sleep. The hot dream had nothing to do with his wife. He could wake her up with leisurely Saturday morning sex or a quickie, but he wasn't in the mood.

Their exchange last night left a bitter taste in his mouth. They had both been tired and overwrought.

He could hardly recognize his wife over the past few weeks. What had happened to the empathetic, yet driven Rachel, who laughed and enjoyed life to the fullest? Where was the gregarious, self-assured woman he had wooed and fallen in love with eons ago?

Silently, he got ready and left for his squash session with his brother. Driving on auto-pilot to the country club in Edgware, he savoured his sex dream, which involved Lauren in an unfamiliar place, in control of her surroundings and him.

The rigorous squash workout and even defeating Adam did little to burn off his energy or restore his equilibrium.

For the rest of the weekend, the hours shot by. James cleared out some stuff in the garage and prepared the garden for spring, while Rachel was still by Tina, probably helping her pack and get the house ready for sale.

All the physical exertion helped him fall asleep as soon as his head touched the pillow soon after 9p.m. He never heard Rachel come to bed. For the first time in what seemed like years, they didn't spend their weekend or even part of Sunday together.

By 7a.m. on Monday, with papers strewn on his office desk, James was just about ready to face Lauren without his body responding, or his face heating as if his dream was written on his shirt for all to read.

His breathing sounded laboured in the quiet office. No phone calls, no one needing anything from him this early.

Concentrate on your work, so much depends on you. He had work to finish before catching the flight to Aberdeen. Remembering that overt twinkle in Lauren's eyes at the pub, looking at his wedding band, now helped bring down his erection.

Taking another swig of his black coffee, he knew he ought to call Rachel to make it all fine between them. But right now he did not care about keeping her happy or about missing this month's chance of pregnancy. He was in the midst of a complex merger, with two major projects unlikely to meet their quarterly schedule. He was travelling to Scotland for work, not just for the hell of it. He had to earn his title and the large salary Acorn paid him.

He shuffled slightly in his seat.

Working together and staying in the same hotel as Lauren—and Mac, of course—should sort the men from the boys.

God help him.

~

Yet another unexciting Monday at the office, Rachel sighed. Admittedly it was a sunnier, warmer March morning but with JT gone for almost the whole week, she wished her days whizzed by like they had in her London agency position. On days like these, she missed the stimulating hustle and bustle of working in one of England's top successful real estate agencies in Central London. She didn't regret foregoing the stress that came with heading her own team in her previous job but neither was she feeling Zen or anywhere near calm.

As a woman of action, thriving on making a difference, she merely felt unfulfilled. And she was never good at waiting.

Her line rang and she picked up her office phone.

"This is Dr. Carter's office. You'd asked us to let you know of any cancellations. We have one on Tuesday, 12th of April, at 1.40pm. Would you like it?"

"Yes, please." JT may be called away again, so she wouldn't contemplate waiting for him at the risk of delaying her next exploratory tests. It could take another few months. "I'll be there, thank you again."

With shaking fingers she replaced the receiver and faced the mess she had made of things on Friday night. With both of them committed to other things, the busy yet frustrating weekend hadn't resolved their rift. This morning, her distracted husband had just about said good-bye with a cursory peck on the cheek, as she still dozed.

But she couldn't blame him one bit when her outburst had been his last straw.

A few weeks ago he would have lavished extra attention on her before leaving even for a night; most fertile time of the month or not. When he was away, she hated the deafening quiet at home and loved his late evening calls, catching up on their days and hearing him say in that low deep sexy voice, "I miss you, darling." But these days he was increasingly withdrawn with his work sapping his energy and attention.

And then she had pushed and pushed.... Why hadn't she cancelled or delayed the dinner plans?

CHAPTER 12

Her boss was becoming increasingly difficult to tolerate, and her thoughts kept veering towards Brandon, who had thankfully not contacted the firm since their last meeting.

Unfortunately this increased Gareth's dissatisfaction with the world and made him more irritable.

Adding to all this, the nagging prickle grew with every day that something was up with her conspicuously absent Abby. Her sister hadn't returned her calls of three weeks ago. She hadn't heard from her for nearly two months. Was her latest boyfriend not the perfect rescuer Abby sought? She would catch her at Café Vert, Abby's trendy vegetarian restaurant in Islington, after work tonight to make sure she was all right.

She quelled her fear for her beautiful, tortured sister. They were all the blood family they had left, and her radar over Abby was almost never wrong. But JT's reminder to let her baby sister live her own life brought back her sense of doom.

Determined to stop the melancholy she focused on the new listings on her screen. But the thought would not leave her.

Had her desperation and impatience pushed away the only man who truly understood and loved her?

Her life may not be perfect but it was relative heaven compared to the current horror Tina and her family were trudging through. Feeling helpless witnessing such unbearable changes in her friend's life, Rachel had spent most of the weekend with her shell-shocked friend, listening to her trying to make sense of what was happening. Having arranged for Tina's boys to spend the weekend with their grandmother, Rachel had typed up and given her an action and prioritization list to help them both start purging and packing up a marriage and a life which had once seemed invincible.

"You're very organized and are excellent in a crisis, Raych." Her father's husky, sad voice replayed in her mind. She hadn't thought of either of her parents for months. But worrying about Abby always brought the painful childhood memories back. Through her dreams, especially when she slept alone. As she would for most of this week.

In her early teens, she had discovered that nothing stayed the same. Happiness was never guaranteed. Mothers ran away with young, smooth-talking contractors, fathers took their lives without a thought to young daughters.

Move forward. She kept herself and Tina busy and moving. Too many times through the Saturday and most of Sunday, Rachel had stopped everything and just held her crying friend whenever a piece of furniture, a book or a silly gift shattered Tina's fragile composure.

Rachel gave herself a deserved metaphorical smack upside the head.

Put your life in perspective and remember to count your blessings before you screw it all up. Who could ask for a more wonderful and caring husband!

She was adamant that she and JT were strong together, despite her screw-up. She was certain they would sort it all out when JT next called her, or at least when he returned home. And he deserved better than her growing obsession. He loved and cherished her but there was only so much a person could tolerate.

Clearing her constricting throat, she focused on her computer monitor and braced herself as Gareth strolled in through the main office doors, holding his neatly rolled umbrella, despite the clear weather.

Stopping by her desk he stared down at her. "I take it Mr. Ross's promised offer has still not materialized."

And a jolly good morning to you, too. "No, but remember he had been called away on business and said that he'd be—"

"So, when do you plan to call him? Perhaps this morning, and make yourself useful? After all, you were his choice to show him around.... Or *was* that a ruse after all? Having a little on the side on my time, hmm?" He leaned in slightly. His generously applied cologne almost stung her nostrils.

"Please don't say those things, Gareth. I'll call Mr. Ross shortly." She picked up the sheaf of fresh listings on her desk and deliberately scanned the details of GRB's latest acquired properties.

Gareth made no move to leave. "And yet not denying it."

The phone trilled again.

"Good morning, GRB Real Estate Agency, Rachel speaking."

"Hello, Rachel." The low male voice on the line was unmistakable. Her heart lurched and a warm blush heated her face.

"It's Brandon." He offered unnecessarily. "How are you?"

"I'm fine, thanks, Brandon." She bore Gareth's curious stare without looking up at him. "I was about to—"

"Have you had a chance to miss me while I was away?" His velvety tone was hypnotically soothing against the familiar sounds in the open office despite the receptionists' voices, the copier and the humming coffee maker to her right.

She pulled the receiver closer to her ear. "I relayed your message to Gareth that you'd be away until today. Please hold on a moment." Putting him on hold and she told Gareth, "Brandon Ross is on line two. Or would you like to speak with him *here?*"

With a sniff through his haughty nose, he strode away to his office.

"Brandon, I'll put you through to Gareth—"

"I'm coming in today to sign the papers for Carrington Drive and then we can discuss further properties over a Chinese lunch."

"Gareth will be happy to go with you but he doesn't care for Chi—"

"You and I, Rachel. It's a business lunch. I'll pick you up at 12:30."

"No. Brandon. *I'll* continue emailing you with fresh properties you may be interested in and *Gareth* will take you for lunch whenever you'd like."

Her boss craned his neck from his desk, watching her.

"I'd like *you* to deal with me." Brandon's words reminded her of their days and nights dealing with each other until sweat and need had...

That was merely sex. Now you know real love.

At her silence, Brandon laughed. "Are you afraid of me or yourself?" His voice did strange things to the hairs on the back of her neck, trickling deliciously down her stiff back.

Counting to ten she stayed silent.

Brandon chuckled again. "Okay, little chicken, put me through."

"Please hold." She transferred the call to Gareth and replaced the receiver. Her breathing was erratic as if she had run a few miles without stopping.

She knew Brandon well enough to know what he wanted. Was he solely biding his time? Well, she was unavailable, despite her growing fear of impending doom, which melded with naughty excitement.

CHAPTER 13

With only twenty minutes to spare James, Mac and Lauren made it to the right Heathrow airport gate. Although it was only an hour-and-a-half plane journey, Mac fell promptly asleep as soon as he settled himself in his seat across the aisle from him.

The silent Lauren sat next to James. There was nothing left to discuss about the impending 3p.m. meeting at the Wellsley Valley site. His breathing was somewhat stifled and the spacious business class seats were too close to each other for his liking.

After a few minutes of typing with her quick red nailed fingers, Lauren quietly closed her laptop and rested her head back. Noticing her far away expression, he wondered if she was meditating like Rachel did after an especially frustrating day at work.

Pushing away at the guilt at not having reached out to his wife, he asked, "Have you got a big family?" What was it about the proximity of an airplane that made people feel obligated to make small talk?

"No. Well, I've got twin half-brothers who live in London. But I hardly see them."

He realized belatedly she didn't particularly care to talk about the topic. "What interests do you have outside work?"

"When I have the time, mainly I like reading the classics, and doing yoga. The gym is mandatory rather than an interest. International and black and white movies and musical theatre. Especially Flamenco or Tango."

"You have a lot in common with my wife, apart from the gym. She enjoys yoga a lot."

"Oh, really?" Again, that aloofness. While many women loved to talk about themselves, with Lauren, any subject outside work brought on poker-face politeness.

"What are *your* hobbies?" She smiled into his eyes. She crossed her long legs and the fitted olive skirt rode up slightly. He kept his eyes on her face.

"I don't have time for much these days, but...I suppose nothing original. When I was a teenager I played the sax in a jazz band. Now I like watching sports whenever I get a chance. I play tennis and squash once a week and sometimes golf. And I like classic cars. You see? The stereotypical male."

"I don't think there's anything typical about you, James." A long pause followed. "So do you also own an antique car or kit car?" The teasing smile lit her face. Her hazel-green eyes looked warmer at such close quarters, the dark lashes accentuating their brightness. He'd never noticed the tiny dimple near her left side of that luscious mouth.

His smile felt forced, glad his jacket covered his groin area, hoping she couldn't see his chest rising and falling slightly. "No, my old Mercedes is all I have. I suspect classic cars would be too high maintenance and expensive for me, and I'm not mechanically inclined."

"So you haven't been tempted to go and buy a brand new Porsche or Lotus or something."

"You mean like a mid-life-crisis present to myself? Not yet." His lip twitched in irritation.

As he looked away from her, she gave that laugh that tinkled softly. She touched his arm, sending heat through his layers of clothes. "I was joking, you know. You're in your mid-thirties, or thereabouts, right? And you're in pretty good shape, if you don't mind me saying something so personal."

"Thanks."

"Does your wife keep you on your toes about your health, I mean? I've seen you at the company gym. And wondered if you enjoy exercising or...."

"I'm not one of those sports addicts who enjoys exercise." He didn't want to talk about Rachel, who admittedly didn't nag him about his health. Unless it affected his sperm-count. "I just do it."

He was aware how Lauren was looking at him. An attractive, interesting man. Him, James, not him the husband, or the boss. Just him.

Was this how his father had felt when....

He didn't want to talk anymore. If she did he would change to a safer subject of work.

"So is playing the saxophone your passion?" Lauren asked.

He shook his head. "I enjoyed it, but I grew out of it, I suppose."

"I love listening to the sax and its mellow tones. I find it quite romantic. I used to play guitar."

∼

Nearly two hours later they collected the hire car, a tinny mid-size sedan, at Aberdeen Airport, and Mac drove North, directly to Wellsley Valley's old plant. After the presentation, the three would rest for the night at the highly recommended local hotel, five minutes away.

James's first impression of silvery overcast Aberdeen wasn't the greatest. With the rain pelting down, he watched the unappealing grey country side through the car window. The herby scent of damp cool air soaked into the car and into his bones.

Forty minutes later they arrived on the narrow gravelled path leading to their destination high on a moss-green covered hill. The sound of the scolding wind and the hazy views reminded him of old black and white movies. The hard edges of the newer granite four-storey structure built on the side of the original three-hundred-year-old Wellsley Valley building was cold and unwelcoming.

Like he suspected the people within it would be.

There were hardly enough windows, making James feel claustrophobic even before setting foot in the place. Mac was obviously of the same mindset. "We have our work cut out here in this dreary God-forsaken part of the world."

The atmosphere inside was as stale and morose as the outer shell had promised, but everyone appeared to be present. There wasn't a smile or a polite expression between the lot of waiting men and women shuffling, standing or sitting in the clammy, fluorescent-lit meeting hall with its tall heavy, black beamed ceilings.

As everyone sat, he wondered if they held rotten tomatoes and eggs behind their backs.

James gathered up his PowerPoint slides on the lone table on the elevated stage with Mac and Lauren on either sides of him. A hush came over the crowd as he addressed the silent audience.

Getting to the last slide, he reiterated about Acorn's short-term as well as long-term plans. "That concludes my part of the meeting. Do any of you have any questions?" He braced himself, expecting a barrage of opposition.

Seconds ticked. A couple of hesitant hands went up and James answered the questions. When he laid out plans for the new equipment to be shipped within the month, a hissing sound and a grating of a chair from the middle of the crowd got his attention.

"Excuse me, sir," The heavy Scottish lilt belonged to a heavy-set, grey-bearded man, his chest puffing up his brown sheepskin coat like a bear ready to pounce. "Bob McThornton's the name, and I've been Project Manager at Wellsley Valley for the past thirty-two years. What makes ye think these changes are necessary? What's wrong with the way we've been doing things till na? We've done very well till ye come along with all these shiny new ideas dreamt up in your London offices." Grunts from around him confirmed he was speaking for many of them.

James looked down from the stage, with Mac and Lauren as his only allies.

But this was why they were here, to try and win as many people over. Relishing the opportunity he had foreseen, he opened his mouth but Lauren leaned closer and whispered in his ear, "May I take this one?"

He nodded. Let her try and he would take over if the tomatoes or eggs started to fly.

Lauren took in a breath, squared her pretty shoulders, stood firm on her high-heeled legs and stared at the challenger in the audience. His balding head shone under the unflattering lights.

"We understand that all this is new and may seem unnecessarily process-intensive, but at Acorn Pharmaceuticals, experience has proven that our products get to the market on average four months sooner with cost savings of up to 12%, when compared with the conventional approach of fifteen, twenty years ago. Let me show you this example."

James watched her smoothly introduce her prepared slides with a couple of clicks, expanding on the facts and backing up her statements. Obviously prepared for the anticipated questions, she shared all the vital and finer points eloquently and persuasively. He was impressed. Lauren had great potential.

After answering another few questions when the crowd stayed silent, she sat down. Over the next hour, the three of them addressed the remaining comments and questions.

As the crowd dispersed, he was glad there had been no

showers of food. But neither were there any converts. Yet. After nearly twelve years in the various executive roles in the industry, he hadn't expected any visible acceptance.

Tomorrow would be Phase Two. Facing his colleagues, James recognized Lauren's sense of accomplishment within her sparkling eyes. As they left the meeting, he followed Lauren, refusing to be distracted by her pert bottom swaying slightly from side to side.

It was dusk when they arrived at the Wellsley Valley Hotel. As they parked, the rain had stopped and it was fresh and still, broken up by their feet crunching on the gravel outside the sprawling ancient castle turned into a luxury hotel. It was surrounded by dark blue-grey cliffs and green hills in the darkening distance. The five-star hotel prided itself on quality service in opulent yet relaxed surroundings and James looked forward to tasting their renowned venison tonight.

The huge ceiling-high smoke-tarnished hearth with a roaring fire in the huge lobby cast shadows over the tall, carved wooden panelling around them. As they registered at the welcoming lobby and got their keys, all James wanted was an invigorating swim to clear his head.

Then after dinner, he would call Rachel and get some much needed rest. Early next morning, they would start the to tackle the complex and emotive evaluation of the plant and its people.

This aspect of his job didn't appeal to him. It required him to lead his team in assessing the performance of the plant and its management, which inevitably led to dismissals and restructuring. He hoped their updated incentive program would motivate the remaining staff to come on board with the new plans.

When shown into the large room with tasteful masculine dark brown and gold décor, with hits of blue-green tartan, James opened his carry-on bag on top of the king-size bed and sought out his swimming trunks.

About to dive into the giant kidney shaped pool, James was

relieved there was only one person swimming in it. Throwing the towel on to the nearest chair he dove in at the deep end. The azure blue of the cool water in the mosaic-tiled pool enveloped and reinvigorated him.

It may have been a few minutes or it may have been an hour later when he finally forced himself out of the pool. Water streaked off him, leaving puddles beneath him, as he reached for his towel. Only then did he see the immobile familiar female form a few feet away.

If he hadn't been breathing deeply from exertion, he definitely was now.

The smiling cross-legged Lauren lounged at a nearby bistro set, her tall glass half filled with ice and clear liquid. The humid air clung to his cooling skin as he towelled his hair. He felt her leisurely gaze on his working muscles as he ambled towards her.

"Delicious," Lauren raised her eyes to his. "Isn't it?" Her eyes still focussed on him, her chin jutted towards the pool.

"Yes. I prefer these natural salt water pools."

She looked amazing in her low cut black swimsuit, her wet, red silky hair smoothed back from her fresh face. Her long legs seemed to go on forever, with those dark red toenails....

He turned his eyes and attention away from her towards the large wall clock way above her. "I'll see you at seven."

"Yes." She lifted her glass with an enigmatic smile in return.

Keep your bloody mind on the right stuff, boy. As soon as he was in the change room, he inhaled sharply. *You can look, but don't even think of touching, ever. In fact, don't even look anymore.*

CHAPTER 14

The intimate restaurant boasted low lights and high-coffered ceilings. The elegant furniture and the ornately carved bar looked as ancient as the well-maintained castle. The atmosphere was subdued with only two couples in the room when James joined Mac at the far corner. Mac's dark head stooped over his nearly empty shot glass.

Lauren soon joined them. Her discreet yet sexy grey-nearly-black dress clung to her curves. He concentrated on the menu in his hands. They ordered and made small talk in quiet voices.

It was nearly nine-thirty when Mac stood up. His paunch looked precariously large over his belted tan trousers. "I think I'll call it a night. See you in the lobby seven thirty tomorrow. Good night." His large face offered a tight smile and then James found himself alone with Lauren in the now empty restaurant. The bottle of Merlot they had drunk with their excellent meal was quietly replaced with another, but James wasn't sure if it was the wine or the company that was relaxing him. Despite the sexual tension, he was enjoying himself.

Because he knew himself. He wasn't like his weak, cheating father. He was made of stronger stuff. And he loved Rachel. He wasn't like the men who took advantage of young women with bright eager eyes, listening intently to their bosses' every word.

"So you still believe you've made the right decision by giving this position a shot?"

"Of course, why shouldn't I?" She seemed surprised.

"But it's so remote, so out of reality here."

"Maybe that's what I like most about it."

"So you don't have any ties, anyone at home?"

"Oakwood or London aren't my home. I was born in Yorkshire and brought up in all sorts of places. There's something earthy about this place. I knew I'd like it. I'd visited Aberdeen with my father once." Her eyes dimmed slightly. She looked away, as if intrigued by the intricate tapestry against the floor-to-ceiling panelled walls to her right.

"I meant a boyfriend or love interest." In the intimate atmosphere it seemed appropriate to ask.

"Love isn't on my agenda, never was, after the way my father dumped my mum for another woman and left us both for her."

"I'm sorry. How old were you? You don't have to talk about it..."

"It was on my seventh birthday." She took another sip of her red wine, swirling the glass in slow movements. "I was told to stay in the car. Scared and confused I saw Mum screaming at Dad outside this big house. He kept apologizing, saying that he loved me but he also loved this woman, and they had a new life now. I never understood why he chose this other pregnant woman over Mum and me. I never saw him again until I was fourteen, at Mum's funeral."

"That must have been so hard for you."

She looked at him and her short laugh sounded bitter. "She found solace in the Vodka bottle, blaming me for my father's sins, for looking too much like him... But I'm sounding like a victim now, and I'm not anymore."

"I'm sorry." James said softly after a few moments. "But not all men are like your father, Lauren."

"Aren't they?" It made James think of his own father, who admittedly hadn't left, just strayed and returned and stayed. "Forget it, I'm sorry. I shouldn't be telling my boss personal details about a history that hardly belongs to me anymore. I'm happy wherever I can use my brains to bring order to chaos. Like you, I suspect. You're amazingly perceptive. It's like your sixth sense anticipating, always one step ahead. And you're so fair with everyone." There was that respect and admiration shining in her large eyes. The past seemed thrown away into the dark night out of the damask curtain-framed window.

"From today's meeting, I know you're more than capable of doing wonders in this plant. I have no doubt you can achieve anything you put your mind to."

"You sound like my career coach." She laughed. The refreshing, thrilling sound returned, more like a delicious giggle coming from behind a closed door. "We're beginning to understand each other now." Lauren held his gaze, "And I appreciate your faith in me."

"You know what you're really getting yourself into. It's so—"

"Remote, secluded, I know, James." She smiled, putting her hand on his for a moment, "I know exactly what I want."

Her expression changed to something more primal. He tried to clear the slight haze in his head. Moments ticked away.

Get up, say good night. Talk with Rachel and make it all okay between us.

But he didn't want to just yet. It was probably the wine, he was sure.

As Lauren got up, he stood too. Turning round to pick up her small bag from the back of her chair she nearly swooned. Glass tinkling against glass on their table instantly alerted James, who steadied her. He held her long enough to help her regain her balance, but the frisson that passed between them was unmistakable.

He tried to erase the feel of her soft, supple breasts against his open jacket.

The real thing, her warm body, was even more tantalizing than any graphic dream.

Her eyes were inviting.

James straightened, widening the inches of space between them. He felt awakened. Despite her femininity, she was almost as tall as he was in her strappy sandals. She smelt divine.

Her soft lips lifted in the corners as she apologized. But was she really sorry about her clumsiness?

"That's what I get for not being a regular drinker." She blinked coyly, letting her low Diana Krall voice trail off into silence. Her laughter bubbled in her throat as she faced him, leaning into him. He wondered what other vices dominated her life. Her lips were so close to his, he could smell the lemon sorbet and the wine on her warm breath.

Because of his erection, it took all his resolve to move away from her casually. His hands itched to feel her.

"Let me walk you to your room." He said hoarsely.

Later entering his own room, he tried to forget Lauren's disappointed expression outside her door a few minutes ago. He felt horny and on edge but he was also proud he wasn't the type to be led by the wrong part of his anatomy.

His watch told him it was almost ten-thirty. He needed to call Rachel and hear her soft trusting voice. To tell her how much he loved her. And apologize for acting immaturely on the weekend.

But reaching for his mobile, he heard a gentle knock at the door.

∼

On Thursday afternoon on 12 April, finally going through the exploratory tests, Rachel tried not to scream out as the blue liquid seared through her insides. She needed JT here to hold her hand. But she hadn't wanted to bother him. She dreamed of giving him good news rather than drag him to more tests unnecessarily.

She scrunched her eyes shut, hardly breathing, praying the dye would travel through her fallopian tubes. She couldn't bear to look at the monitor to her left above the operating table she lay on. What if it all gushed out of her?

Dr. Carter's soft voice was explaining what he was seeing, "Try and stay calm, Mrs. Windsor."

Last year's laparoscopic procedure had been successful. Having eliminated the cysts and clearing her tubes, her painful, heavy periods were physically more bearable.

Could this agonizing procedure shed more light on whether her years of suffering with endometriosis since her early teens were really behind her inability to get pregnant?

Rachel knew she was holding the nurse's hand too tightly. But she couldn't help it. Her marriage, her future depended on the results.

She waited for the agony to subside and for someone to explain what they saw.

Why was everyone so silent?

"Stay perfectly still, Mrs. Windsor." The nurse suggested gently. "It'll soon be over."

Rachel's tears escaped down her temples, as she swallowed the lump in her throat and the rising apprehension.

Oh JT, I need you so much.

CHAPTER 15

"Hello again, Rachel." The low male voice was unmistakable. Rachel's heart lurched in quite a different way this time as she looked up at the tall figure by her desk. Heat rushed up to her face. Brandon's sexy aura exuded an air of sinful indulgence, throwing off the industrious atmosphere of the office.

It was a warm Wednesday, and the midday sunlight glinting through the floor-to-ceiling windows cast a golden light over his imposing frame. He wore a smart dark suit, with a creamy yellow silk tie against a white shirt. She had rarely seen him in business attire in the old days, resenting his casual dress on their dates.

Now almost breathless, she admired how handsome and in control he was over his surroundings. With his black hair sleeked back, he looked like he'd just stepped off a GQ magazine. He'd probably have won the Sexiest Man Alive status. Confident that he was irresistible.

"Gareth has the papers for me to sign." He said softly as he offered his hand in a firm handshake.

She became aware that Megan and Tracey, the receptionist

and the office girl, were watching them. But Brandon didn't appear to notice anyone else.

He wouldn't free her hand.

"Yes. But he isn't back until—"

"I know. I thought we could go for a quick bite to eat." Brandon finally let her hand go. So he was here despite her determined refusal.

"As I explained, I can't." she saw the girls slowly edging closer. "I'll get the contract for you and here's the printed list of the properties I emailed you."

"Wouldn't you rather sit in a quiet restaurant and share a bowl of won-ton, sesame prawn toast and Peking duck with me?"

Flattered at his persistence and that he remembered her favourite dishes, Rachel was about to admit she no longer liked Chinese and realized it was James who didn't care for it.

Brandon leaned over her desk, his smile dazzling. "It's only lunch. Who knows, you may even enjoy yourself." His still amused green eyes dared her. "I promise not to talk about anything which makes you uncomfortable."

She *was* being stuffy. It *was* only lunch. And it was good for business. She unfurled her fists on her desk, smiled at her childishness and stood up. "Okay, a quick lunch would be good. Thank you."

Suddenly she was ravenous.

"That's better." He helped her with her raincoat and she grabbed her handbag. As he followed her towards the door, she smiled at Megan, gave her a few instructions, and added, "I'll see you soon."

"Take your time." Megan's ever-ready smile included Brandon as he held the door open for Rachel. He then flashed the girls a gorgeous smile.

Taking in a deep fresh breath, the prospect of enjoying his company brightened her mood: A temporary interlude out of her reality.

She hadn't anticipated seeing Gareth but the cantankerous balding man was strolling towards them, an instantly curious expression lighting his long face. With his immaculate charcoal grey three-piece suit, and perfectly rolled up black umbrella he looked like he belonged on a 1950s movie set.

"Ah, Mr. Ross, I see you convinced Rachel after all—" Gareth smiled.

"Yes, we'll be discussing some more properties over lunch. I'll sign the first offer later." Brandon dismissed the beaming Gareth.

"Have a nice time."

Brandon acknowledged Gareth with a short wave. Discreetly touching her arm, they continued in the opposite direction from her boss.

Once out of earshot Brandon said, "So, from successful broker with a team of ten people to here? Why?"

"The short of it is that I didn't want the stress...as JT and I want..."

"A baby. So local job, less stress?" He said softly.

"In theory. Gareth was quite reasonable and flexible when I first started working for him."

Brandon leaned closer and asked, "Is he as pompous as he looks?"

"These days he's worse, and he seems to think I'm after his company." She grimaced.

"Because he knows you're better than him."

"Let's not talk about him."

"No problem. We'll just talk about us." He laughed at her expression. "I'm kidding, will you please relax?" He smiled as they entered the dim confines of the restaurant, with exotic mouth-watering aromas welcoming them. The peace was a great contrast to the noisy high street just behind the silk and wood screens encrusted with jade carved exotic birds.

As they sat in a secluded corner, Rachel fidgeted in her seat. "Brandon, I accepted your—"

"Lunch invitation." He looked into her eyes, that playful smile too sexy for words. "I'll keep my word but first..." He sat back, his eyes twinkling at her. "I have to say, you look even more beautiful than I remember. Those big brown eyes...how could I have taken 'no' for an answer when you broke up with me? Okay, I know you're now a happily married woman, so I promise I'll stop." He patted her hand, sending warm tingles through her body, her heart doing a ping-pong jive against her ribcage. She had an urge to hide behind the long menu card.

"Good, remember that, because I'm quite different from who I was ten years ago, Brandon, and if you think I'll be as easy—"

"You—easy!" He laughed out loud, making the two businessmen from two tables away turn to look at them. "You must be thinking of someone else." He leaned closer over the intimate table and added softly, "We're two people having lunch and discussing business. And believe it or not, I *am* capable of enjoying a woman's company without trying to rip her clothes off." An eyebrow rose.

Her face and neck warmed. Despite the swirling in the pit of her abdomen, she willed her tense shoulders to loosen and relax. "I'm sorry, Brandon." She smiled.

Maybe he had changed. She remembered the last time they had been to a restaurant together. Their last meal before she had broken up with him.

The last straw had been when they had entered his local Chinese haunt in Muswell Hill. Upon entering it he had let go of her arm, as if afraid to see one of a long line of broken-hearted old flames. Making her wonder if he was waiting for someone better, different to come along. Was she cramping his style?

As clearly as if she was watching a video of their conversation, she remembered that night when she'd broached the delicate subject of her needing more commitment from him. "I can't just be there for you when you want to share my bed and whenever *you're* available. I want much more."

He had shrugged casually, avoiding eye contact. "What's wrong with things as they are?"

"You say you love me, Brandon." Rachel's calm voice had betrayed none of her inner turmoil.

"Yes, I do. But it's only been a few months, why not continue enjoying getting to know each other?" He'd looked around the crowded restaurant discreetly, as if embarrassed by the words usually shared in his or her bed. "And now's not the time to talk about this." His bright eyes had roamed to the table behind Rachel and from the knowing arrogant expression on his face she knew there must be a mirror or an attractive female looking his way. The lopsided Elvis grin was ready to charm the coldest, emancipated woman. Just like it was doing right now. Was there a beautiful woman who was staring at him from behind Rachel?

~

Pushing away her past meanderings, Rachel studied him over the menu, and wondered if a leopard really could change its spots.

What's the difference? Nothing to do with you anymore.

Relieved that he appeared to have accepted that she was truly unavailable, and that she had her own life now, she would take Brandon at face value.

Before long, she was laughing at his witty stories, enjoying his company and the cold white wine. It had been too long since she had enjoyed authentic Chinese food, which over the past years she only ate with Tina and her other friends before they had got too busy with motherhood. She felt alive and exuberant in the presence of a man who had inspired that all-consuming recklessness in her early twenties.

Without effort Brandon made her feel sexy, carefree and feminine. Babies weren't even on her mind right now, she realized.

Thinking of her incommunicative absent husband, she wondered if she would mention this lunch to him.

Not caring about time or going back to the office, something within her shifted. Where was that sense of impending doom, that prickly feeling, which had helped her keep Brandon at arms' length?

CHAPTER 16

APRIL

Reliving the guilty pleasure of yesterday's lunch with Brandon, Rachel checked on the simmering pot of French onion soup, one of JT's favorites. Its scent transported her to Paris for a moment. Then her mind filled with a disturbing yet mouth-watering vision of Brandon clad with only a deep chocolate brown towel precariously around his hips. The coarse, dark hairs on his broad chest thick and manly veering toward his... The fantasy was more tantalizing than the creamy wine and mushroom sauce she was stirring. Her nipples taut against her bra and cotton top. The languid sensations forced her to lick her parched lips. She reached for a glass and filled it with cold water and drank deeply.

Phew, it was hot in the kitchen.

Think of JT. He would love this meal. After the fragrant onion soup, she would serve the chicken morsels on a bed of aromatic rice and sugar snap peas and beans.

But her thoughts kept returning to Brandon, even though on

the most part he had kept his word and hadn't mentioned their history together.

And that was where these fantasies belonged. In the past.

Rachel hoped her husband's mood had improved after their many days apart. He had apologized the other night and from his deep voice she knew how much he missed her as he told her he loved her. His work was obviously at the forefront of his mind because he had sounded strained.

Hearing the front door open and close made Rachel's pulse skip erratically. As JT entered the kitchen she nearly dropped the wooden spoon.

She recognized the expression on his face, intermingled with something alien, dangerous in his tired eyes and the set of his stubble-darkened jaw.

He strode towards her with purpose. The determination in his grey eyes heated her even more than her earlier musings. The bubbling aromas of the cooking dishes were ignored. Her heart thudded and blood rushed to her ears as he ate up the final step between them and reached for her. She let the spoon fall on the granite counter and welcomed him. Wrapping his arms around her his firm warm mouth followed where he was staring; at her parted lips. He kissed her urgently, deeply as if he had returned from a decade-long absence and every moment apart had been agony.

Groaning, he pulled her even closer into himself, his erection confirming that he needed her this minute.

"Rachel…" He said gruffly, "I missed you so much. I love you… I'm sorry about—"

She shook her head, "No, *I'm* sorry, JT."

They had spoken on the phone last night, they hadn't seen each other for five days, yet he looked at her as if it had been years. His tense bear hug brimmed with promises of unbridled passion as she nuzzled against his familiar warmth, his strength. Eyes closed, he deepened their kiss. Sighing, his mouth moved to her cheek, grazing lower to the hollow of her throat and collar bone. He tugged at the hem of her too warm top, disconnecting his mouth from her long enough to pull the barrier of clothing over her head.

The static crackled between them, entwining them.

As his lips roved from her neck to the crevice between her breasts, anticipation melted the pit of her stomach. He raised her skirt, caressing her hips, buttocks, her thighs, all the time kissing her throat, shoulders and exposed parts of her swelling breasts.

Breathing shallowly, she became half conscious of the darkness outside the windows. She gasped realizing that JT intended to make love right here, right now. Imagining him picking her up on to the counter like they had done years before.

She whispered hoarsely, "JT..."

He looked at her as if through a fog, his breathing rough.

She wriggled round in his hold so she could turn off the flames under the bubbling saucepans and Dutch oven with shaky fingers.

As she turned to him he asked gruffly, "Here, lights off? Or the bed."

"The bed." His need for her sent shivers through her ready and hot body. She gasped as he effortlessly picked her up against his rising and falling chest.

She felt tiny, feminine and so desired.

Arms around his corded neck, she welcomed his grating jaw against her cheek and temple. She inhaled his familiar male scent of car leather and faint body cologne that still clung to him. His fast heartbeat sounded like an ancient drum as they escalated to their haven.

Rachel felt his growing erection as he gently let her feet touch the bedroom floor. A sliver of light from the hall illuminated JT's form as he made quick work of undressing, while his glazed eyes concentrated on Rachel's face and contours.

Freeing herself from her remaining clothes, she enjoyed the play of his muscles until at last he stood naked and fully aroused as he pulled her into him. She enveloped her arms around his neck and their bare flesh wherever they connected made her hungrier for him.

His breath warm against her ear, he licked and sucked at one of her erogenous spots on the side of her neck. Goosebumps multiplied as his mouth lowered to capture one breast, then the other, with his slow yet persistent tongue and fingers.

Her nipples hardened to attention, her breathing becoming faster.

She forked her shaky fingers through his thick hair, manoeuvring his head to catch his mouth with hers. Honey-like need swelled within her womb. She was wet and ready for him.

Turning her to face him just as her knees weakened, he picked her up and lay her on the bed against cool, silk-soft sheets.

Not breaking eye contact, he dipped his head to her breasts again, further lavishing his tongue around each areola and the curves of her breasts. Worshipping them until she wanted to scream with agony and pleasure.

Then, trailing hot kisses towards her quivering tummy, he circled her navel until she was ready to die from the erotic tension within her.

When his lips descended to her pubic bone she held her breath.

Fevered and on high alert, she knew she was about to combust.

Parting her legs with sure, caressing hands, JT's fingers on her inner thighs, his tongue found her moist centre. He licked her as if she was an exotic fruit he had hungered for all his life. Their gazes connected until her pleasure took over everything. The desire in his smile and eyes told her to let go of her remaining self-control. That JT was king of her body and soul.

Laying back, she groaned and finally let out her breath, melting against the now too hot sheets as powerful waves of pleasure obliterated further thought. She surrendered to the ecstasy. Thrumming with unrelenting rapture, at the mercy of her husband's hands and mouth, her deep, breathless moans escalated into panting cries. Again and again, until she needed him to join her in the bliss.

As she drew her elastic, shaky body up to massage the sides of JT's head, willing him to come to her. Slowly rising above her, leaving a trail of hot kisses on her jellied belly, her ribcage, right breast and throat, he stared down at her. Supported on his elbows he kissed her deeply and again lowered his mouth to one over sensitized nipple then the other.

He groaned, apparently in the same volcanic pleasure world.

"I need you inside me, JT... Now..." Her pleas came out desperate.

As he effortlessly leaned over her fully, his erection so close to her centre, she anticipated another full-fledged climax they would share, this time together. Breathless, she luxuriated in the feel of his hard torso, rising and falling so close above her. She kneaded his straining biceps and welcomed him deeper, wrapping her quivering legs around his waist and lower back.

Breathing roughly, at last he entered her. Slow, hard and steady. She gasped. How had she forgotten how wonderful it was making love with JT? She felt tears at her temples at such completeness in being in his arms. Hungry hands explored his sinewy shoulders and his back as she inhaled his distinct subtle scent, which was now mingled with their lust and need.

She tightened her legs around his taut buttocks, needing him so deep inside her that he would be part of her. As she matched his every urgent thrust, his pleasure-filled eyes scanned hers as if to confirm she was in the same heaven he was, braced for their mutual fulfilment.

Once again letting herself go, moaning out his name, she climbed the tip of the most exhilarating orgasm she had ever had, riding wave after joyous wave of ecstasy.

"Yes, JT," she whimpered. "I...love you so much."

JT's laboured breathing matched hers. They were attuned to each other's needs.

He looked down at her as if seeing her for the first time in years with that open adoring gaze before he kissed her again. Then he groaned and arched his back as if in blessed release.

Loving his heavy, pulsating body in and over her, breathing was overrated right now.

"I love you... too." He said almost inaudibly into her ear as their rollercoaster ride eventually calmed.

Seconds passed and rolling beside her, JT pulled her tighter to himself. Their sweat-sheened, vibrating bodies sated, for now.

Rachel couldn't remember this frantic desire and heightened level of passion between them since the beginning of their marriage. Smiling, her eyes shut, she nuzzled deeper into her husband's embrace.

Life outside this room didn't exist.

CHAPTER 17

Feeling tired but accomplished after the Wellsley Valley trip, Lauren pushed away her sense of shame at ending up outside James's hotel room door, and instead focused on the positive feedback James had given her on their flight back. After wading through the local Safeway to stock up on fresh produce, she welcomed the solitude of her quiet house.

With almost all the stuff put away, she noticed that she'd missed a call and pressed the keys to listen to the voicemail. She had to sit down as she heard her step-mother's calm voice, "I thought you should know that your father had a mild heart attack this afternoon." The message went on. "If you'd like to speak with him, you can call King Edward Hospital. The number is...." Marilyn gave the number, and after a pause added, "Or if you'd prefer to see him, he's hoping to be discharged tomorrow and be home later in the afternoon. In the meantime, you may call at home or on my mobile—" Lauren turned off the rest of the message. She still had no intention of calling or seeing either her father or Marilyn.

She was glad to have missed the opportunity to acknowledge

receiving the satisfying news: The booming powerhouse that was her father wasn't so invincible after all.

Maybe nature would beat her to seeing him defeated.

Bloody good! She shoved the milk into the fridge with unnecessary force. If he died, it would free her from this constant drive, this longing that had become her sole and trusted companion.

In the middle of the night, a scream awoke her. She sat up, her heart pounding hard, having thrown the sheets off her clammy body. Feeling her wet, hot cheeks with trembling fingers she realized it was her guttural scream that dragged her out of a haunting dream.

She had stood by a large granite head stone, with her coat collar up against the wind in the grey winter surroundings. Her ashen-faced father with blank eyes was in the open casket being lowered into the grave.

But instead of her laughter, heart-shattering wails rang out from within her, joining Marilyn's and the twins' cries. Even now as she padded to the kitchen for water, her sadness gnawed at her insides. It wouldn't leave her.

The aloneness had never pierced her insides so hard. She had absolutely no one she could trust or talk to.

Vincent with his young bad-boy vibe came to mind. Sure, he was all about fun and his next adventure, but she was only twenty-eight, nearly twenty-nine. He was entertaining and made her smile. That was an achievement in itself. And after the way she had opened herself up to James and he had gently but firmly refused her advances, and with tonight's news, she had to shake off this funk.

She wiped the fresh tears off her face and despite the early morning hours, she picked up her mobile and texted Vincent, "You can come over if you'd like." And before she could change her mind added her address and sent it.

*T*alk about great make-up sex. There was no drug more powerful than love or sex.

Smiling, Rachel stretched her aching but sated body between the sheets, like a pampered cat. She was glad today was her day off. Marvellous, languorous relaxation permeated through her, and with the scent of their sensual hours still on the sheets, she relived last night's passion.

Although they had never gone to sleep in an argument before, neither had they made such all-consuming love. Being in JT's arms had felt familiarly satisfying and yet different. It had felt fresh and exciting. Who needed a fantasy lover when her husband satisfied all her needs?

Brandon couldn't have been further from her mind last night.

Now slowly opening her eyes, Brandon crept back into her mind, but only a blurred shadow of his face remained.

This was the one: the night of passion that would finally fill the baby room. Of course, she hadn't dared voice her thoughts to JT. Neither would she mention her painful invasive tests she had endured at Dr. Carter's clinic earlier in the week. The results were due in May. If they shed some positive light on why she wasn't getting pregnant, it would be worth going through the pain, as well as having something to tell JT. She prayed...

Stop it. She had done this too often, like so many pacts with God, and suffered repeated dejection at the end of each cycle. She was not a quitter, but JT was right, she had to be patient.

Remember, this obsessiveness had upset him.

Although she had loved his making-up tactics, this morning he had been preoccupied again, getting ready in the half-shaded bedroom.

She sighed and slowly closed her eyes, unwilling to face the morning that wasn't that sunny after all. Her mobile rang in the silence. She reached for it, hoping it was JT, irrationally dreading it was Brandon. How could he know her number?

Honestly, guilty conscience.

It was Abby on the line, sounding groggy, unlike her usual self.

Instantly Rachel sat up in bed, fully alert in fight or flight mode. "What's wrong? You sound..." *Please, please not another accident.*

"I'm okay, Raych. I need you. Would you come...for me?" Abby sounded sleepy. Nearly nine-thirty in the morning was not that early with her sister's restaurant schedule. "I'm not at home, but don't worry."

"Of course I'll come. Where are you?" Rachel kept her voice steady, and bit her trembling lip when Abby told her she was in Whittington Hospital.

CHAPTER 18

Somehow Rachel managed to navigate through the inner city's remaining rush hour chaos, finally found a parking space, paid for it and reached Abby's hospital room forty-five minutes later. She was a nervous wreck but was determined to keep cool for Abby's sake. She would wait for her to tell her what had happened this time. However, opening the door to the two-bed room and registering her sister's pitiful state—with her left arm in an awkward cast, and the heavy dark smudges under her haunted, swollen eyes—Rachel forgot her resolution.

"What happened, Abs? Your arm, and..." Was that a black eye? She cringed.

"I'll explain later." Abby looked so broken, pale and fragile, it squeezed Rachel's insides, pushing away all her self-absorbed thoughts. She carefully leaned toward her sister, gently kissing her dark head.

The vivid image of the last time she had collected Abby from this hospital sent currents of pain darting to her temples, nearly blinding her for a moment. Insistent nausea rose but she hadn't eaten today.

Breathe deep and concentrate on Abby.

"Do you think James would mind too much if I stayed with you—for a short while?"

"Of course he won't."

"Would you still ask him?"

Rachel nodded. "Sure. Don't worry about anything, Abs."

With her sister's knack of attracting the wrong type, Rachel suspected Abby's boyfriend of seven months was to blame for Abby's sorry state.

When she had met Rick that once at Abby's restaurant, the sexy, tall sandy-blonde haired, twenty-something man with a cold blue stare had sent fear through her. But Abby had been all smiles and full of excited love. After the earlier weeks of short 'hello-yes-everything's-fine' phone calls, Abby had stopped calling. Rachel gritted her teeth at the guilt of not having been more proactive and checking in on her sister.

"Thanks, Raych." Abby offered a stiff half-smile, averting her eyes to the characterless cream walls of the confining room. "For being there for me...always." Tears shone in the eye that was not almost closed shut with horrible blue and bloody mounds of nearly transparent flesh.

Balling her hands Rachel seethed inside.

Having turned their Dad's and Uncle Abe's café into the trendiest successful restaurant in London, Abby was so intelligent, so why did she get herself into these situations? She adored her sister but seemed unable to help her, protect her.

How long would Abby go on this way? She could have been killed.

"I'll go and see the Doctor and find out when we can be on our way."

Abby slowly nodded and then her troubled expression changed to one of peace, her breathing becoming slow and rhythmically shallow. Swallowing down the lump in her throat, Rachel tiptoed out of the room.

~

Slowly waking up, Abby tensed as familiar fear trickled through her as she became aware of her sterile surroundings. A large hand kneaded her limp arm, which was not in a cast, and she had no energy to cringe away from the intruder.

"It all got too much for me. I didn't mean to do it, honest." Without moving her head, she squinted through her good eye in Rick's direction.

He sat by her side sniffling, shaking his head.

Summoning strength, she pulled her hand away from his and shut her eye. The excruciating pain in her shoulder and neck trickled hotly down her spine.

Letting out her held breath, she longed to lose consciousness again.

Bile threatened to choke her at hearing Rick openly crying.

"How dare you come here? Just leave me alone." She said softly, but clearly.

"I'm sorry. I love you, babe." She refused to look at him as he added, "Please give me a chance...I can see a counsellor with you—"

Abby opened the one eye through which she could still see and he stopped speaking. Her hatred must have been patent on her face. Paling, his eyes lost their vibrant blueness.

"Get the hell away from me. Take your stuff out of my place right now and stay out of my life.... or I *will* press charges." Despite the agony breathing let alone talking caused her, she slowly added, between shallow breaths. "If you come near me again, I swear I'll kill you... I mean it... I'm not afraid of you anymore... Right now I care for very little." Her mouth was so dry and her throat burned. Everything hurt.

Rick got up, fists by his sides. She closed her eye and waited for his footsteps to confirm he was gone.

Thinking she was all cried out, she lay deeper against the

pillow and fresh tears heated the back of her throat and leaked out. Pain throbbed within her head.

From Rachel's first reaction, Abby could only imagine the horror of what she looked like. She didn't care to see herself in the mirror anytime soon. Her 'exotic beauty' had always been her curse, and this further proved it.

How many weeks would it take for her to regain some mobility and return to the restaurant?

Had Rick stormed out of her life for good? Or would she have to take legal steps?

With more tears, unsure and not caring about anything, she moaned, "I wish I was dead."

∼

Outside the door, Rachel stood shaking in silence. She had caught the exchange between her sister and Rick before he had stormed out of there. At her sister's voice, Rachel had frozen and stepped back from the door and had heard enough to confirm that Rick was the bastard who had done this to Abby. And he was still free to roam the streets and spread his venom.

Abby's monotone voice reminded Rachel of the incident three years ago, when Abby had become involved with a sweet-talking married man with too many vices.

Three months later, Abby had ended up in hospital with a miscarriage.

Rachel's gut roiled with familiar fear. At that nightmarish time, she had gently rocked Abby's clammy body, with tears streaming down her own face, hearing Abby crying, "I wish I was dead."

Like she had just heard her sister whimper.

CHAPTER 19

Watching the quiet and polite JT at the dinner table, Rachel tried not to take his aloofness personally. He usually enjoyed and complimented her cooking, especially her poached salmon with buttered fingerling potatoes and asparagus. But looking at her distracted husband, the passionate night of love forty-eight hours ago may have been a mirage, borne out of her desperation.

Pushing the negative vibes away, she turned her attention to the too skinny and pale Abby, who sat awkwardly beside her, delicately poking her fork at her still full plate.

There had been no explanation between Rachel and JT on the phone yesterday before she had brought her bruised sister home from the hospital. Abby could stay for as long as she needed or wanted. JT had made it clear years ago; family was everything.

Abby's two previous long visits were too painful for Rachel to contemplate. Even though it was Saturday, JT excused himself and disappeared into his office.

Rachel sent Abby up for a long bath in the guest bathroom. "It'll do you good, Abs."

Rachel was relieved to be left alone to clear up.

Although she understood about business pressures, she frowned at JT's growing preoccupation with his work. Remembering Brandon's tenacity—current and from years ago—she started making the unlikely comparison of the two men's approaches to business.

Maybe they weren't so different after all. Both were driven, knew what they wanted, and went for it.

Slowly her mind drifted back to the pleasant lunch sharing Peking duck with him. She gripped the dirty plate too tightly.

Enough daydreaming.

Tina's phone call yesterday had added to her guilt. She had been lunching with an ex-lover, while her sister and best friend were suffering through all kinds of hell. Having settled Abby in the guest room to sleep the afternoon away, Rachel had rushed to be with Tina.

"You're such a good friend, what would I do without you?" Tina had said for the umpteenth time over the past weeks. Her blue eyes had lost their sparkle, her long hair no longer the silky blonde she took so much pride in. A far cry from the happy-go-lucky petite blonde of a couple of months ago.

The nearly three-year-old Justin ran in from the hall with a beheaded Barbie doll, offering it to Tina. "It bwoken." Tina took her old doll in one hand and its golden head in the other, studying them through more tears.

"Thorry, Mummy. Dustin thorry. Don't cry." His big brown eyes—so like his Daddy's— widened, his lower lip quivered as Tina hugged him. Rachel would have joined them if not for her wits about her. Distracting the boy to run and find Nanny with a promise of a nice snack, Rachel made a strong cup of coffee for Tina and a herbal tea for herself. She wouldn't wallow with the poor family who needed her to stay positive, focused and strong. She prayed that once they moved into their smaller place next month and left all the sad memories behind them, Tina and the boys would get some semblance of eventual peace. "It's a small apartment, but I don't care. And at least I'll be nearer to Mum and you."

The enchanted castle in Tina's fairytale had obviously been built on quick-sand of deceit and infidelity. With fresh shame, Rachel reminded herself that she and JT still had unexplored options to have a family, but most important they truly loved one another.

But once trust was broken or love was gone, that was the end.

"I don't know how we're going to manage but one way or another I bloody well will. I'll have to get a job, but I won't have a nanny to help. Mum says my lawyers should squeeze Andy harder for financial support. But I can't stand looking at him. And yet it's so empty in the bed... I can't imagine life without—" She broke off, grabbing her disintegrating tissue and scrubbed at her swollen eyes. "How can I still l-love someone who's such a prick?" Tina gritted her teeth, obviously experiencing the next stage of grief, which Rachel recognized too well from her father's last months of life.

Giving Tina two fresh tissues, Rachel held her tight against her shoulder, rocking her like she had so often consoled Abby. Tina's sobs racked through her slim form, as if she was mourning her husband's death.

How easy it was to break up a happy home, a living breathing relationship with one wrong decision. With an innocuous lunch here, a touch there.

In a rare moment of clarity, Rachel vowed not to have any further contact with Brandon, and she ought to shred his card into tiny confetti.

No more egoistic interludes of playing single or fantasies of 'what if's, even in the name of business. She loved JT, and no matter how busy or aloof he was, soon he would be the same attentive, witty and fun man she loved. Hadn't her own crazy-busy real-estate career taught her how hectic and all-consuming work could become? She would make a fresh effort to ask and listen to JT about his work and his ambitions. They used to do that so often, and she would support him through this difficult period of reorganization at the company. The responsibility lay fully on his shoulders.

She *had* been too consumed with longings for a baby, instead of nourishing her love relationship. What poor Tina was dealing with brought much needed perspective to Rachel's own life. With two small boys and no recent work history, Tina was on her own. Imagining the next horrible months ahead for her friend, Rachel decided to talk to Gareth about giving Tina a chance at his agency.

It shouldn't have taken her friend's horrible situation for Rachel to take stock and fully appreciate her own life and marriage. She buried away the guilt of keeping secret her escapades and looked forward to next month's specialist appointment for her results. She dreaded and yet couldn't wait for it to come.

In the meantime, Tina and Abby needed her, and in his own way, so did JT.

Turning away from the now empty and clean sink, through her peripheral vision Rachel noticed a soft fluffy shadow standing by the kitchen door. She wiped her hands on a tea towel and turned to her sister with a smile.

CHAPTER 20

"Did you have a nice bath, Abs?" Her insides warmed at the sweet picture Abby made with her long black hair combed smoothly back. Her large blue eyes so like their father's made her look like a teen rather than a nearly twenty-six-year-old.

Rachel's snowy thick bath-robe touched Abby's ankles. Trying not to cringe at the blood-shod black eye and the cast supporting her left arm, Rachel realized nothing detracted from her vulnerable sister's aura of innocence. "You should have called me, I'd have helped you shampoo your hair."

"It was fine, and the big plastic bag was a good idea, Raych. Thanks." Her eyes thanked her for more than the hot bath. "I can't wait for when I can have a fully submerged bath, though. And even though I've slept the day away, I was nodding off in the tub." She stopped in mid-yawn as if it hurt too much.

Abby padded silently in Rachel's bed socks to the biscuit jar, reminding Rachel of their childhood.

"Your floors are always so shiny and clean, I don't have to worry about being told off like I used to for dirtying my socks." Abby smiled wanly for the first time, further brightening when she offered her a mug of steaming hot chocolate she had kept hot on the stove top. Abby's dimples, one of the few things they had in common, deepened in her sullen cheeks. "You never forget, do you? How do you know I haven't grown out of hot chocolate?" She sat at the table and wound her fingers of her good hand around the big cup.

"How can anyone grow out of hot chocolate?"

Abby shrugged her good shoulder slightly and then grimaced

"You make me feel like a little girl again." Her voice told Rachel she wanted a hug.

It was given freely.

"You are a little girl, sometimes." Rachel smelt the fresh shampoo on her sister's damp head. "We both are sometimes." A sigh rose from deep in her chest and she closed her eyes, savouring the warmth, her sister's love. Their eight year age difference had made Rachel the surrogate mother while their parents had openly acted out their volatile rollercoaster of a marriage. Despite their tense and unpredictable childhood, some of its aspects still made Rachel wistful. Like their alone time with Dad, and those four years they had lived with Grandma Nancy after he had… died. She pushed away the anger that threatened to resurface at how both their parents had abandoned them. Their only relatives on their father's side lived in Australia and had never been forthcoming before or after Grandma Nancy had passed away. Seventeen-year-old Rachel had taken over looking after them both.

"Is everything okay between you two?" Abby asked.

"Yes, of course. Why?" Rachel was surprised that in her state Abby had picked up any vibes, however wrong they were. "I feel the tension between you and James." Abby dunked a Digestive biscuit in her hot chocolate while still watching her lovely, generous sister.

"It's nothing, really. He's just got a lot on his plate at work. But we're good." Rachel averted her eyes from her, making Abby wonder what she was keeping from her.

She wouldn't meddle, knowing how private her sister was. "I know I don't look like I can help right now, Raych, but since I started seeing the psychotherapist six weeks ago—" She saw the surprise and a spark in her sister's eyes as she continued, "I realize how right you were about talking about your emotions. If and when you want to share anything, I'm here for you. Even if it's merely to listen to you. You've always been there for me, for Tina, and everyone...." Abby studied her face seeing the tiny quiver of Rachel's chin, and the moistness in her brown eyes.

"You're so adorable. Thank you for that, Abs. I love you." Rachel touched her hand tenderly and said, "But you're here to recuperate. For as long as you need.

CHAPTER 21

Abby sighed. Obviously Rachel wasn't ready to bare her soul to the black sheep of the family, who always found trouble, and who could blame her? "Why are we so different from each other, Raych?" She stared wistfully in her chocolate drink. "I wish I had your determination, to know what I want and go for it. That's all I've ever wanted: Mr. Right or at least someone romantic and sincere who'd marry me and adore me. And have a nice home like this."

Yet they both knew that she shied away from men who could genuinely offer her that. Yes, she saw that James adored her sister, and he was the whole package for Rachel, but Abby kept veering towards guys who made her insides quiver. She braced herself at the long road ahead of her, with her therapist's help. Having braved to seek out Dr. Karl Muller's help had exacerbated her imploding relationship with Rick, but she would have still been trapped in her own flat, her own life had she not done something drastic to keep her sanity. Facing the bully had almost cost her life and she was determined to learn how to break the chains of repeating her mother's history and grow out of her destructive patterns where men were concerned.

"You're only coming close to your twenty-sixth year, Abs. I'm the one who's getting up there. By my mid-twenties I had gotten my fingers burnt more times than I'd care to admit to, especially to my little sister." Her voice was light, but when Abby glanced at her, Rachel was studying her. "And when you were twelve you swore you'd never marry as long as you live." Rachel smiled, adding, "You were most passionate about that."

"I don't remember that." Abby frowned, the familiar discomfort within her ribcage returning in full force. "I suppose it's not surprising after the example... Mum and Dad showed us."

Abby saw Rachel's eyes widen at her rare referral to their parents' messy and tragic marriage. "And... Once I can bear to let him see me like this, when I go back to my therapist I have to start facing many things in order to turn my life around. And I'd also need your help to put some of my missing pieces of our childhood memories together."

Rachel nodded, "Of course. Although she was too ashamed of her appearance to see Karl for this week's session, at least here she had a safety net, feeling somewhat secure, with new hope for her new future.

"And sure enough you changed your mind when the hormones kicked in. With your looks it was plain you'd have no problems in getting any guy you wanted."

Abby buried her chin deeper in the folds of the warm towelling robe, revelling in its freshly washed fragrance, the smell of her sister, her unconditional love. She didn't see beauty when she looked in the mirror, especially when facing herself in the bathroom mirror earlier. "Right now I feel hideous and like death warmed up." Thankfully, the deep darkness dragging her down a few days ago was lifting somewhat. "Thank God for you."

"You poor darling. At least you're out of it. You're safe and sound here." Rachel leaned in from her seat and held her. Abby wallowed in her embrace, letting tears escape down her face even if it hurt in so many different ways.

Abby's sigh hurt. "I know I've said this before, but I really want—need—to change. I'll do whatever it takes to get Rick truly out of my life. But that's not all. Without Karl's help I know I'll keep making the same mistakes. And I'm the only one who can make these serious changes. I'm so sick and tired of going for the same kind of guy."

Her sister watched her face carefully, as always without judgement. Abby almost wailed with shame and gratitude.

She swallowed, "I've only seen Dr. Mueller a few times so far and without him I'd still be… It may take a while, but I'm determined to get myself sorted out." Abby's chin lifted proudly. "He's so very kind and understanding. I can really trust him. He's like a father-figure, you know?"

Rachel touched her free hand and squeezed it. "He seems very kind and experienced. I'm very glad, and I'm proud of you, my darling. It's time you saw your own worth."

"Thank you." After a moment Abby had to ask, "What about you, Raych? You're really happy, right? You've—almost—got everything you've ever wanted, so far?"

Rachel nodded. "Of course. I had some tests last Tuesday."

Rachel averted her eyes again at the hint of another taboo subject, confirming there was still no success on the baby front. Abby knew she'd be the first to know when it happened.

"I'll pray you'll get some good news. It hurts me to think of someone as maternal and giving as you still waiting. And here I am, adding to any stress…."

"Of course you're not. I told you everything will be fine." She spoke fast in an upbeat tone.

"Still I feel rotten about my own self-absorbed stuff. Getting you involved again, you're so lovely, Raych. I'm so lucky to have you…"

Rachel gave her a dismissive wave. "I'm always here for you, remember, Abs, and you've got every right to feel low right now.

You're leaving behind the hell you've gone through and we'll both concentrate on moving forward, right?"

She saw the urgency in Rachel's eyes. Could she read her morbid thoughts of a few days ago? Abby nodded, "I love you and your constant optimism."

"We both have a lot to be grateful for."

Then Rachel updated her on Tina and her family. "It made me feel so guilty and self-centred about obsessing about wanting a baby. It helped me put things in perspective, to remind me what's really important in life. Just like you need time to heal, and to have the psychotherapist help, I also need to be patient."

Seeing the shadow cross her sister's face, Abby asked her about Café Vert.

"Everything's under control. I've been in touch with Kevin and I'm going in tomorrow." Rachel reassured her. Abby breathed a deep sigh of relief and froze in pain. It took her mind off her injuries as they talked about Rachel supervising at the restaurant for the next couple of weeks.

"I know you're busy with your own work and with poor Tina, but I know you can do the work with your eyes closed. I'm sorry I got you involved again... And one of these days I'll make it up to you."

"Stop apologizing and start healing, sis! And that's an order." Rachel hugged her again, careful not to hurt her fragile sister.

CHAPTER 22

MAY

For the past weeks since their return, James had successfully avoided being alone with Lauren. Her regular trips to Wellsley Valley kept her on top of things and she kept him and Mac updated every day. The details of the next steps of the merger and preparing for next month's company gala also kept his team busy. When their paths crossed, Lauren was her usual cordial self, which helped him put down her unprofessional lapse outside his hotel room to too much wine on that first night in Wellsley Valley Hotel.

It had taken so much more willpower than he could have anticipated not to get lost in those inviting eyes. Her lips had almost been his undoing. But he had reasoned that in addition to being tipsy, she must have been lonely or bored.

In those few short moments he kept a tight rein on his emotions, knowing that many faced temptation but not everyone went down the dangerous path toward scarred, if not obliterated marriages. Fantasizing in their hungry minds, with no repercussions and 'emotional affairs'—he believed women called them—were one thing. Giving in was quite another.

He was different from the rest. He was not like his father. *He* took his marriage vows seriously. As he knew his wife did, too. Nothing was worth ruining not only his marriage but his entire life and career.

He had been one proud man when after staring at each other, he had slowly shaken his head with a regretful smile.

Now, here Lauren stood in his office, looking pale, almost shell-shocked. "I'm afraid I have to resign." She laid down the small white envelope on his desk.

"What?"

At his sharp tone she looked straight into his eyes. "I'm sorry, but it's for personal reasons."

"If it's about Dave making it difficult for you..."

At this Lauren shook her head.

After a moment he said, "I don't understand, can you elaborate?"

Lauren's eyes misted. Was she on the brink of tears? Her lower lip trembling, she sighed and nodded. "I think it's only fair to be open with you as you've always been so kind and respectful towards me..."

She sat down and said, "I'm pregnant." Silently she watched him.

He tried not to show his surprise. Then he waited for more.

"It happened on our return when I got a message from my step-mother that my Dad was in hospital with a heart attack and although I'd always imagined I'd be glad to hear that he'd got his come-uppance after the way he'd treated me and Mum... instead it shook me to the core." Her lower lip quivered again and this time tears fell down her cheeks.

She lowered her head and continued. "I—I made a mistake. This is in confidence, of course. But I finally said yes... and I hooked up with one of the guys from manufacturing."

James remembered a couple of months ago when he'd seen the young, buff, good looking Italian standing by his Harley, talking intimately with the non-committal, polite Lauren.

He knew why he didn't like Vincent. He had the same cocky attitude as Brandon, Rachel's ex boyfriend. Even from the few moments of connection at the French restaurant, James had seen right through the arrogance and the spoilt guy who went after whatever he wanted, and got it whenever he wanted it.

"And now the only way I can take care of this is by having the baby and giving it up for adoption."

Deep pain struck within him but he kept his voice calm, "Are you sure you can't keep it?"

"No... Out of the question, I'm not the maternal type and there's no room for a... baby in my life, ever."

Something hard kicked him in his gut. How cruel life was. Why did God let women like his sister-in-law and this confused woman get pregnant while Rachel continued suffering?

And what if he had given in to his fantasies and he had gotten Lauren pregnant?

What a bloody stupid thought!

He balled his hands and tried to breathe through his frustration.

Stay professional.

"I'm so sorry you're going through this, but may I suggest that you consider staying on and we can work something out?"

She looked stricken, "Are you sure? People talk and I think it's simpler all around if I leave as soon as possible."

He nodded, "I know that. Take some time to think about all this while you're at Wellsley Valley, but know that you're a very important part of this reorganization, and my offer stands."

"Thank you, James. I won't be coming back for the gala, and after I'm back I'll take a few personal days off... I'm seeing a specialist." She looked away from him and he wondered if she was considering getting rid of the baby despite her words.

He didn't really know her, after all.

His insides clenching at life's unfairness, he stared at his watch. It was past six and he had hoped to get home in time to eat with Rachel. Yet again he had missed another opportunity to catch up with her.

No matter what was going on at work he would make time for his generous natured wife. He missed their talks, their dinners together and their fun easy life before the need for a baby took over everything else.

He wished he could share what was going on here, but he didn't want to dwell on work once he got home and he definitely wouldn't burden her with any of it. He needed her. And he knew she needed him too.

~

For the past three weeks Rachel was in a haze, pushing away her morbid fears. This morning, when she awoke alone yet again, she was sure what the specialists' results would confirm. That *she* was the problem and would never be able to give JT their own baby.

The frustration grew when her appointment with Dr. Carter was delayed due to an emergency surgery that had demanded his expertise. She had to wait for next week. With every day her gut also warned her what it would mean for her marriage if her fears of the results were confirmed.

When had this happened?

Reliving the day of the tests when she had wished JT had been there to hold her hand, Rachel prayed that the agony would be worth it.

The increasingly preoccupied JT looked leaner these days. The strenuous work was obviously taking over his life. Because he had never been away from home so much. Unless the gulf between them *was* due to her obsession.

Her fear and resentment grew. She was almost glad of his absence, on some level. Would the tests prove what she suspected and feared? Was *she* to blame for them not getting pregnant? Because since the diagnosis of his low sperm count James took all the various vitamins and supplements and still made time to exercise to stay in good shape.

She wouldn't contemplate their options if the impending results did confirm that she was... she pushed the word 'infertile' out of her mind.

Adoption was not on JT's agenda, and she didn't dare broach the subject.

A crazy, erotic vision filled her mind. Making urgent love with her old flame and getting pregnant. Letting her imagination run wild made her want to burst out laughing. Or was it crying?

Something had to change but she didn't know how to break free from this stagnant situation.

Everything was different, Rachel sighed. Where was her JT, her lover, her best friend with whom she shared everything? Especially after their wonderful, sexy night upon his return almost a month ago?

Her depressed friend Tina was hating living alone with her two children in the flat near her parents. The good news was that Gareth had hired Tina at the office on a part-time basis. "As long as you train and supervise her." He had said in his autocratic way.

Most of Rachel's other friends believed her life was on an even keel while she waited. Neither Mark nor Annabelle had called her since last month's dinner. Seeing herself and her marriage through their eyes made her feel an even bigger failure. That dinner, on the night that had started this downward spiral, or had it just brought everything to the fore?

Although she was ovulating, she knew making love was not on JT's radar at all. Despite his lack of interest in anything but work, she would try tonight. She missed her husband.

CHAPTER 23

Getting ready for bed, James felt the tension in his gut quadruple as Rachel said, "I know you've got a lot on your plate, JT, but I was hoping that..." He was sure she was about to tell him that she had ovulated. He wished he was up to making love to his beautiful wife, but despite his best intentions earlier today...

"Are you so tired you can't even look at me now?"

He turned to her. "I'm sorry, Rachel. I was preoccupied... it's just work...."

Rachel stood before him in the pale cream silky camisole he loved on her.

"Is it about Abby, do you mind her being here?"

In the light of Lauren's news a few days ago, he tried to shove away the memory of how devastated Rachel had been after the previous hospital episode three years ago with Abby's miscarriage, which had left both sisters needing consoling and support.

He shrugged, "You know I don't mind." He put his watch down on his nightstand. Abby wasn't any trouble and within a couple of weeks she planned to move to her new almost completely renovated place above her restaurant. He appreciated how she stayed late at her café on the weekends to give them their own space at home.

"She needs patience and understanding." Rachel said.

"And you're giving it. Now let's get some rest." He saw the disappointment in her eyes but suddenly he was too tired.

"It's not just about Abby, is it? Am I missing something? That night when you returned from Scotland and we made love it was all so perfect... but since then," she seemed to be searching for the right words.

He gazed up at her, amazed at how attuned she was to him. "It *was* perfect, Rachel. It's solely work. Can't I just be tired?"

"These days you're always tied up with something or other."

He could tell she was trying to control her inner turmoil. And he couldn't add to it by mentioning anything about a pregnant co-worker who didn't want anything to do with the embryo growing inside her.

He turned away from her, picked up his pillow and beat it twice to puff it up. Glancing back at her, he straightened and sighed deeply, "There's some stuff going on at work and also I suppose I'm worried about you over doing it." After a beat he added, "It's always the same pattern with you and Abby, when you constantly keep bailing her out like this... The dreaded phone calls and you coming to her rescue and picking up the pieces." James hated the image of Abby like a broken winged bird when she first came here last month. "And I remember just how it affected you at the last 'unfortunate' incident. I want you to make sure you're not stressing about her too much. Is that fair enough?"

"She's my sister and she needs me, us." She frowned. "Everyone can make a mistake, even you or I. No one can guarantee what type of person we're really getting involved with. She's just not been as lucky as we are." Seeing how upset she was getting, James reached for her and hugged her. "I know. I'm so tired I'm not being as understanding as you deserve." He kissed her and sighed again, looking into her beautiful eyes. "You're one of the nicest people I know. You make me realize what's truly important."

And taking an example from his wife's kind nature, he committed to be more present with her and Abby. And he would also try and find a way to help Lauren in her unfortunate situation.

"Come here, darling." He pulled her gently into himself and sighed against her temple, kissing it. "I want to feel skin against skin and just forget about everything else." His brain started to feel relaxed and his body responded to their closeness. He needed her more than anything else and they would work through everything together. "I love you, Rachel." He mumbled as he kissed her and she held on tightly.

~

Am I going mad or is it my imagination? Rachel couldn't quite put her finger on it, but despite their intimacy and his words, she felt JT was keeping something from her.

What was happening to them?

She missed those beginning years of their marriage when JT used to entertain her by sharing the quirky happenings at work. When they still talked about their work, she felt proud that he took her seriously, that he deeply cared about her and saw value in her ideas.

Now, as she lay wide awake despite her own tiredness, she admitted that her obsessiveness was behind his aloofness, and who could blame him? After the past long weeks while he worked late into the evenings, she spent more nights alone with the TV or a book for company. Abby was ready to return to her own place next week but she wasn't sure if JT really did mind her staying with them.

Rachel had not told him about Thursday's long-awaited

specialist appointment. She prayed that she would have some good news to share with him.

And she would do whatever it took to make them a family. JT would have a baby to come home to every night. Not like these days, with only an edgy, nagging wife and a sister-in-law he didn't understand.

Did he still love her as much as he had before, or had her obsession scarred their marriage after all?

CHAPTER 24

Rachel wasn't surprised that JT forgot to mention this Saturday's company gala. Simone, his super efficient personal assistant of seven years had called her yesterday wondering if she had misplaced her choice between the salmon or steak dinner for the party. When Rachel had asked him last night why he hadn't mentioned anything about the event, he had groaned and apologized.

Especially now with the low morale at Acorn under the shadow of changes, she knew that celebrating the charitable initiative would bring welcome relief. Acorn Empower Awards Gala honoured excellent non-profit organizations that had impacted the critical health of the community over the past six years since its inception. Rachel hadn't been sure if it had been delayed or would be cancelled this year.

"Perhaps he doesn't want me to go with him," she said to Abby, now trying to enjoy their delicious lunch on one of her sister's rare days off.

"That's ridiculous, and you know it. He's *busy* and overworked. It's a tough position and I've seen how he puts his whole self into it all."

"I know." Because he was distracted at work, she still hadn't mentioned next week's specialist appointment when she would finally get the test results.

The sunny window at one of their favourite cafés in Bond Street allowed them to watch the world go by. After the past week's downpours, today was a perfect May day. Looking forward to Saturday's company do, Rachel knew exactly how she would style her honey-brown curly hair. The diamond and pearl drop earrings, JT's sixth wedding anniversary gift, would be perfect accessories to go with the royal blue dress that was in the bag at her feet.

Rachel had loved her own reflection in the boutique's mirror. The sexy dress made her feel chic with its diamante strap on one shoulder and a long slit half way up her right thigh. Abby had convinced her to buy the sexy number on this rare shopping spree. When was the last time Rachel had tried on new shades of makeup or taken interest in a new mascara wand that claimed extra sensuous long lashes?

What had Abby said? Swallowing her last mouthful of the spinach and goat cheese salad she asked, "You're going to Israel?"

"Yes, Eilat. I just need time away, from everything..."

Rachel lay down her fork neatly on her plate without taking her eyes off her sister's pale but beautiful face. "Is everything all right? You haven't heard from Rick, or anything, have you?" She didn't want to overreact or pry.

"No, everything's fine on that front. Don't worry, Raych." Touching her hand Abby's smile reassured her that she was really on the mend.

"I need time to relax, away from everything… it's lonely at the flat." Since moving back into her now redecorated flat Abby had admitted that she felt odd, afraid to be alone. Rachel couldn't blame her for no longer feeling at home in her revamped apartment after the rebellious parting mess Rick had left behind. Both in tears, the shocked sisters had stared at the destruction. He had ransacked Abby's beautiful place, shredding her modern, custom cream sofas, and leaving mirror and glass shards everywhere. The pale, shaking Abby had stared at the chaos, which had sealed Rick's chances of future reconciliation: at best nil, and at worst impossible.

After bringing in the special cleaning crew almost immediately, Abby had forged forward with her new life.

"So you don't mind leaving the restaurant in Kevin's hands?"

"After the great job you did while I was... absent? It'll be fine. You're amazing, I still don't know how you could juggle everything with your work, at home and helping Tina. *And* you managed to rearrange my inventory documents and organize the new ordering system. And your advice about me hiring an assistant: spot on. I don't know how I'd managed before. Thanks again, sis." Abby smiled brightly. "I know Kevin can handle things on his own for three weeks, but would you... pop in a couple of times?"

"Of course. And what about missing your sessions with the therapist?"

She saw her eagerness in her blue eyes, "Karl said I must make sure I'm not escaping for the wrong reasons. But I need to get myself back on the road to feeling normal, healthy and happy. If I can ever feel that way again."

She was very hopeful as Abby updated her on how well her therapy sessions with Karl were going. "That's so great to hear, Abs. And I'm glad that you're regaining some of the weight and your peace of mind."

Over the past weeks her sister looked and acted more like the happier girl-woman Rachel loved to see. That lost expression in Abby's haunted eyes had almost all disappeared. Glad of the distraction, she was now helping Abby renovate and transform the two large spaces above Café Vert. One of the flats was being turned into an art studio, while the other would become Abby's new abode.

Rachel smiled at her effervescent descriptions about where she planned to set up her easels and new art materials in the new studio space. She felt inspired by this more positive, mature and stronger Abby. "Going away sounds lovely. I wish I could go, too." She sighed again.

"Why don't you?" Abby enthused.

"No, I'd never go on my own without JT." Though she was sorely tempted, because of his preoccupation and working crazy hours, she couldn't just up and go on an exotic escape as if she was young, free and single.

"How's it at home these days?" Abby sipped her lemon ice water.

For a moment she considered opening up to her, having no one to discuss anything about what was happening—or not happening. But she said, "I'm sure it'll all settle down soon. I'm getting the test results next Thursday. Who knows? There may be new options." She hated voicing the hopes that seemed impossible right now. And it hadn't helped when Dr. Carter's assistant had refused to divulge any further information, explaining that Dr. Carter wanted to see and speak with her. "Go and have a good rest, and don't worry about anything at the café. When are you going?"

"Tomorrow at three-fifteen. I wish I'd known about the appointment. I'd have come with you. I'm sorry. I'm never there for you—"

"Abby, don't worry, I'm okay. And we're here together right now. When are you back? I'll pick you up if I can."

Abby nodded. "I plan to return in around six weeks...Wow that sounds such a long time...I know it'll be so hot there, but I don't care. And I can always cut it short."

"Don't worry about the café, I'll keep an eye on it for you."

"Thanks, Raych. I feel guilty I'm leaving you but I hope you get some great news soon. Whatsapp me, okay?"

Rachel smiled and nodded.

"If James is too busy why can't you come even for a week? We could enjoy the swimming and eating delicious kofta, hummus and pita bread like we used to... and read books and not think about work... or anything."

"Sounds heavenly and extremely tempting." But she couldn't escape reality. "Maybe I'll convince JT to go away somewhere together for a couple of nights."

Even though she had planned to go for the results on her own, now she felt sad and lonelier than ever.

It would take a miracle for JT to notice her even in that gorgeous cocktail dress on Saturday.

CHAPTER 25

As the elder brother, James always made a point of listening and advising Adam when asked for any guidance but today he found it almost impossible to focus on their squash game and his frustration boiled over to such an extent he had to apologize and explain. "Sorry, Adam. I've a lot on my mind and it's catching up with me."

"Care to share? You know I'm a good listener. Got a feeling last time at Mum's it's getting tougher for you and Rachel..."

After a second's hesitation James sighed, threw down his damp towel on the bench beside him in the thankfully-empty change rooms. "She's become more distant since we had a... tiff of sorts a few weeks back. I think she's trying not to add to my work pressure. I don't know how else to help her. In addition to my low sperm count, with her issues with endometriosis, I feel..." He almost said impotent. "I feel at a loss at how to be there for her."

"Would you consider adoption as an option?"

"Of course I would, but I know how much it means to Rachel to have our own." He understood why she yearned to at least give it their best shot to have their biological child, so she would feel a better mother than her own had been. Shame gnawed at his impatience with her that night after the dinner party. It now seemed as if it had happened years ago.

"It's bloody hard, I can only imagine, and I don't blame her with the insensitive way Mum pushes you both." Adam shook his head as he stood by the shower cubicle. "Danielle and I felt dreadful that night." He shook his head.

"I can't blame Mum either, she has a right to enjoy what she's always wanted. But I don't have the heart to even broach the subject with Rachel. We used to talk about everything, but these days she's always out helping either her friend who's just got divorced or at Abby's restaurant. Don't get me wrong, I don't mind that she's keeping busy, but..."

The silence grew.

Adam grasped his shoulder and looked into his eyes, "Is there anything I can do to help? Really, there must be something."

James shook his head. "Thanks, and I appreciate the ear and sympathy. And everything will work out somehow." James smiled and hugged his brother. "Now let's stop sounding like a bunch of gossiping women." He hit Adam's back. "Now let's get cleaned up, and I fancy a beer. You game?"

~

Is this how desolate and afraid Tina had felt at the beginning of her marriage's end? Rachel gritted her teeth, seeing no end to JT's aloofness.

As she got ready for tonight's gala, she yearned to have the old, romantic JT back; the positive, loving man she had taken for granted. She missed their long talks. When he used to care about her opinions and work advice.

When had that changed?

She prayed that the impending test results would bring good news despite her gut fears. At this stage it was their only hope.

Once they had a baby and they were a family it would help JT clarify his priorities.

Or was it too late? And hadn't she condemned others for bringing a baby into a rocky marriage?

No. Never say die. They were different and they would find a way to reconnect, and soon. Any couple that was as close as they once were—she reminisced about that spring Sunday night in JT's arms by the romantic fire—and prayed to recover that bond once more.

But how?

No negative thoughts allowed. She would enjoy tonight's Acorn Empower Awards Gala and hopefully make JT proud to have her by his side.

Getting out of the shower, JT seemed to grow irritable. Rachel's impatience grew. She couldn't remember ever seeing him this nervous or edgy. She understood that there were probably people whom he planned to let go of as part of the restructuring of the company, and perhaps felt awkward having to socialize with them. She had yet to hear his address to the nine hundred employees.

"I still can't find it, Rachel." Came the muffled voice from his closet.

"It's where it always is. Here." Rachel picked up his favourite yellow and gold silk tie from behind the others and handed it to him.

"Thanks." He grumbled. He had the same response when she told him how much she loved the new cologne he was wearing. Was that a new dress shirt, too?

She donned on her lovely dress, hoping he would notice her in it. She put on her blingy, extravagant high-heeled beauties, which had cost nearly as much as the dress.

Helping her zip up its back, he continued fiddling with his second cufflink.

"So what do you think, JT?" She had never had to ask before.

"About what?" He glanced at her sideways.

She was fed up with his frowning, cloudy expression. "Really, JT?"

He turned, studied her, and took in a deep breath. He sighed and seemed to take in her presence fully. Was that a grin? He looked so handsome when he smiled. "You look good enough to eat, Rachel. Beautiful." He neared her and placed a small kiss on her forehead. Then he strode out of the bedroom, once more appearing preoccupied.

She supposed a peck on the head was better than nothing. She looked forward to seeing JT's secretary, Simone, as well as some of the staff whom she had met at previous annual parties. Maybe they would be more forthcoming than JT, about what was happening at the office.

As they entered the lavishly decorated, expansive banquet hall, Rachel got an uncomfortable feeling.

JT excused himself and disappeared. Greeting each other, Simone was vague and avoided her eyes, although they had always enjoyed discussing mutual subjects in the past. They made small talk and discussed how well the gala was organized and how gorgeous the balloons and flowers were all around the huge space. But when Rachel asked about how it was going at work on an everyday basis she saw Simone's shoulders rise and her eyes flit away from her. She fiddled with her drop earring and said, "Well, as you can imagine it's really hard on everyone." Simone smiled and then said, "Oh, excuse me, I just want to say hello to...."

When the applause introduced her husband to the podium, he seemed raring to go, to update and reassure the gathered crowds. She knew how thoroughly he had prepared for this but wondered if others could see the underlying strain behind the smiling tycoon's persona.

From JT's powerful speech, which encouraged and appreciated all the employees' hard work and commitment, Rachel gleaned some more information, but strongly suspected from the somewhat forced jovial response at the end of his address that they—like Rachel—had hoped for more in-depth clarification about the future landscape of Acorn. Instead, JT deftly moved on to the awards section of the evening to celebrate the excellent contributions of the many charitable organizations they were honouring tonight.

JT finally joined her at the table for the amazing four-course meal. She watched the people around her and felt something was off, but it only confirmed the undercurrent of the incredible pressure everyone was experiencing.

While the magnificent dessert tables were set up on the perimeter of the left side of the hall, JT excused himself again.

David Andrews caught her eye and she made her way to him as he smiled.

His sunken eyes took her in. "Hello, Rachel, you look so lovely." The smiling, forty-something man seemed much older than she remembered from last year. "Thank you, David. How are Monique and the children?"

After a long moment of silence in a monotone voice he said, "Monique and I have been officially divorced for the past three months." He was no longer smiling.

She felt her face grow hot. "I'm so sorry, I didn't know. JT's been so busy and... he never mentioned it."

"No, I'm not surprised. He was supportive when I'd needed to take the time off when... before and during the ordeal, but lately he's been, well...."

She didn't know what to say, suddenly feeling part of a tribe where wives were outcasts. Again aware of the fragility of marriage. "How's the new promotion going?"

Again there was a pause. "I didn't get it. Anyway, Scotland isn't an ideal place; too far from my kids."

"But, the last time I—" She stopped in case her proverbial foot in her proverbial mouth made things worse and more embarrassing for David.

"A lot's happened in the past three months. I had stiff competition. One minute I'm going, the next minute I'm staying. And to think, I trained her myself."

Rachel frowned and tried to quell the chilling fingers of dread rising up her spine. "Whom?"

"James didn't mention the stunning and ambitious Ms. Mitchell, either, I see." His tight smile made the prickles crawling up her body even more pronounced. The unease that had been triggered at their entry now heightened.

"Is she here tonight?" She swallowed down inexplicable fear. But before David could reply, JT rushed to her side.

～

"Rachel was just asking about whether our new Director of Pharmaceutical Development was here tonight. I'm sure she's exactly where James wants her to be." Pausing, his gaze turned from James to Rachel. "In bonnie Scotland at Wellsley Valley, weaving her magic, no doubt." Dave's benevolent expression couldn't hide what James had suspected. What perfect timing to show his resentment towards his executive decision over three months ago.

He saw Rachel's look of confusion war with something else. Was that eyebrow arching at the inconsistency of his behaviour and late nights at work in the past few weeks? Was she putting two and two together and ending up with a completely wrong equation? Damn, if Lauren had been right after all about the wisdom of keeping her on. More importantly, how could he explain his relationship with Lauren without adding more stress on his wife? Without somehow feeling responsible and guilty....

In a way, he was glad Lauren was at Wellsley Valley this week. Clearly, from how many of his members of staff had looked at him this evening, he was on thin ice. His address about updating and congratulating those present had been accepted with politeness and reserve.

What else could he expect? The powers that be above him were pushing for further redundancies. To them, people were merely numbers, and he was the executor—or was that executioner?—of their demands. His people held him accountable for the successes and disappointments. As the Americans would say, the 'buck' definitely stopped with him.

But after the dinner and dancing, as they starting driving back home, what worried him even more was his silent wife beside him in the car. From her resolute expression as she stared ahead at the road, he could tell she was on edge.

"The politics is catching up with people, as you can imagine." He said.

She nodded and then glanced at him, "Is there anything you need to tell me, JT?"

"Like what?" He *could* say, *Lauren Mitchell is pregnant and I'm giving her brotherly advice, but I've not mentioned anything about her to you because I don't want to hurt you. Because as much as I'd have preferred you to take the specialist's advice and stop trying so hard to have our baby and not even dare mention adoption all those years ago, I know how much it means to you to have our own biological offspring.*

"Anything you... think I need to know."

"It's a really pressured and complicated time right now, but there's nothing that you need to worry about. I'm okay, and *we're* okay. I promise. Once October comes, the work load should definitely ease up." He knew three more months was a long time to ask for her to wait. Instead of burdening her with how the strain of having to let more hard-working people go for no justifiable reason, he grasped her cold hand and looked at her for a moment. "Why don't you choose a place... anywhere you want to go, for end September? I've missed our time together, and I know it's damned hard on you. I'll make it up to you, and soon."

She nodded. He felt her studying him. But she stayed silent. Once again, Rachel seemed aloof, distracted.

It didn't help knowing that he ought to broach the subject of Lauren sometime soon. Before misunderstandings made things even more complicated.

CHAPTER 26

As Rachel sat with clammy palms on her lap, a stunning, tall redhead gracefully entered the waiting room. Hearing her husky voice talking to the receptionist, Rachel was certain the woman had never waited for anything in her life. There was no wedding ring and Rachel wondered what she had wrong with her.

Why should she have a problem? Maybe she was like the other four women in the waiting room, all with various sizes of baby bumps, lucky to be pregnant. Perhaps she was a choosy career woman who had decided to have a baby alone.

No reason for the animosity toward a complete stranger.

The redhead sat in the empty seat next to the small magazine table on the other side of Rachel. She recognized the woman's expensive seductive perfume, which smelled so uniquely different on this woman. She oozed a composed and self-assured energy.

Those ample breasts were too perfect to be her own.

James would love those breasts, that lithe, well shaped body, those long legs. Was she going crazy? Her husband was a workaholic—temporarily—not an unfaithful pig.

To distract herself from her edginess and negative thoughts,

Rachel reached for the Chatelaine at the same time as the redhead. The immaculately dressed woman's soft laughter sounded low, like a female Jazz singer's.

She offered the magazine to Rachel.

Within her beautifully made-up hazel-green eyes, Rachel gleaned an approachable young woman who was probably in her later twenties. Her eyes sparkled like she was about to reveal a great joke. A few light freckles underneath the sheer foundation on her patrician nose gave her an endearing, almost vulnerable quality. Her model-like high cheekbones were flawless, apart from the laughter lines around her perfect mouth. She smiled at Rachel.

As they studied each other, Rachel's first impressions changed. Just like that. She sighed and said quietly, "It's always a nerve wracking time when I wait here."

"Sounds like you come here quite frequently." The woman offered. "I'm sorry, that sounded all wrong." She bit her lower full lip.

"Oh, I know the specialist very well by now." Rachel grinned aware she tried—unsuccessfully—to make it sound trivial, comical almost.

After a beat of silence the woman offered her hand. "I'm Lori."

"I'm Rachel." She smiled back. They talked easily, and before long she was telling her about why she was here and her inability to get pregnant, making it sound a temporary hindrance, and not something which had been an all-consuming issue over the past five years.

After a moment, Lori took in a deep breath, let it out and said softly, "I took a pregnancy test for a joke really, I was only a week late. That's nothing new with my erratic cycle, and I couldn't believe when it proved positive."

"Oh, that's wonderful—" Rachel enthused, and then added in quiet tones they had both adopted. "Isn't it?"

"It would be, but I'm not the mothering type at all. Never will be. My work is all that matters. Besides, I'm not even involved with anyone. A one-off... mistake, which should have never happened." A sad expression mingled with anger crossed Lori's beautiful features. "I don't know what I'm going to do." Then added, "Years ago I was told that I could never get pregnant, and that if I did it could be dangerous. Apparently since I was little I had a heart murmur they couldn't do anything about. And my blood pressure isn't as it should be. My maternal aunt and grandmother died in their forties from genetic heart disease." Then looking at Rachel, whose concern must have shown, Lori apologized. "I'm sorry. Maybe it's this place, and maybe it's your understanding, but I've never discussed these intimate things with anyone. And especially with..."

Rachel was sure Lori had nearly said, 'someone who can't have children', but instead the woman added, "Someone I just met."

Rachel saw that this outwardly cool and successful woman wasn't as brave and worldly as she appeared, needing love and reassurance like anyone else. Lori reminded her so much of Abby. A more self-assured and mature Abby.

Her heart went out to her. "I understand. It's very hard to go through this life-changing stuff without support. Sometimes you need to talk to someone from the outside."

Those large eyes shone. "You're very kind. Your husband's very lucky to have you."

Rachel grunted under her breath. "That's not what he thinks at the moment." She tried and failed to make it sound comical.

"How long have you been trying?"

"Over five years."

"And what are the specialists suggesting now?"

"This test result will confirm whether IVF is an option. But I suspect my endometriosis issues are the main problem. I've been having pains and long periods, since my teens. Paradoxically what can help alleviate the symptoms? You guessed it, getting pregnant. But the way things are between us at present...I couldn't even ask him to come today. I'd not expected him to turn up for the actual tests." She sighed. "So I'm hoping for a miracle." Embarrassed about sharing so much, she asked. "What about you, have you told the man about it?"

Lori shook her head. "No, I suppose I will, but it's up to me at the end of the day. Isn't it always? For all the freedom of modern life, women are always the ones saddled with the burden of carrying and having babies."

I wish I could have that burden. But Rachel smiled at the woman who still had a witty sense of humour despite her equally dire situation.

"As my Grandma would say, 'Have faith, and you'll get your answer.' Bloody much use that's been," Rachel said.

Lori laughed softly, sympathy shining in her eyes. Despite their opposing situations, they had clicked with each other so naturally.

A sharp pain tugged at her heart at the injustice of life, and Rachel tried to erase the painful memory of Abby in hospital with a miscarriage three years ago.

To stop tears from embarrassing and betraying the real depth of her turmoil, she opened the magazine in her hand and studied the black and white close-up of a muscle-bound young man holding a small chubby baby in the crevice of one muscle bound arm. It took Rachel's breath away. The love and tenderness in the male model's face was almost her undoing and she caught her lower lip between her teeth. She could imagine JT with a baby in his bare arms. A few months ago, this picture would have touched him the same way. Today, she wasn't so sure, despite his reassurances that everything was good, that work pressure was totally to blame for his long days and preoccupation.

They hardly seemed together these days. Not only had they not had their romantic Sunday dates with baths or slow showers for way too long, they were hardly even eating together. Every day she was losing him.

Rachel felt Lori's gentle touch on her arm. "I'm sorry, I've upset you. Here we are in these two completely different predicaments, and I should have been more sensitive and seen this from your perspective."

"It's not you." Rachel sniffed as she fished for her travel tissue pack in her bag and dabbed at her tears. "It's been the longest three weeks of my life, waiting for these results. So much is riding on it... my life and my marriage." Her smile wavered then faded.

"If you're finished before I am, could we get a quick cup of coffee afterwards?" Lori asked.

Tears welled up in her eyes at this offer from a total stranger. When had she become so totally alone? "I'd really like that. You're very thoughtful; thanks."

"Believe me, it's selfish. You're the kind of person I'd consider myself very lucky to have as a friend."

Touched, Rachel smiled and prayed for some miraculous news she could share with Lori after the impending specialist meeting. They could then celebrate some new way forward and she would have something to celebrate with JT, too.

But if there was no hope... did she really want it confirmed?

She could hardly breathe. "God, I wish I was with my sister on a beach somewhere right now, instead of waiting here. I don't want to be brave anymore."

"Miss Oliver," called the receptionist. "You can come through now."

"I'll see you later." Lori touched Rachel's hand again and she nodded. "Good luck," she said softly and watched the nervous woman being led away by the nurse.. The young woman with such a life-changing dilemma seemed so alone. Who did she have to help her while dealing with options for her unplanned and unwanted pregnancy?

Why was life so cruel and randomly unfair?

CHAPTER 27

*R*achel didn't know how much time had elapsed since coming out of the specialist's claustrophobic office, when a gentle hand touched her shoulder. Numb, she slowly looked up and recognized Lori's concerned face.

"Oh, no, Rachel. Are you okay?" Her soft voice carried urgency.

No words came. Rachel tried again, shaking her head. "I—I don't know. No."

"Let's get out of here." Lori helped her out of her seat and out of the building as if Rachel was a fragile invalid.

A while later, she didn't know and didn't care where she was as she looked around the coffee shop.

"What happened? What did they say?" Lori asked.

Silence.

"You look so pale, Rachel… you want to drink this tea and then I can take you home?" Lori paused. "You don't have to talk about it if you don't want—"

Rachel stared at Lori's pale face through stinging tears. Blinking them away she said, "All these years there had been some hope. But now... My uterus is... The endometriosis... I have to have a—a hysterectomy."

Dr. Carter's frown had not been a good start when he had asked if she was sure she wanted to talk about this now without her husband present. She had started to shake inside and then outwardly.

Feeling Lori's eyes on her, Rachel said, "I can never c-conceive or carry a child. There are too many cysts and it could prove fatal if I delay further... and JT won't even consider anything else." Feeling the stranger's arms around her, Rachel closed her eyes. Had she known this all along and that was why she hadn't told JT about today's appointment? Whimpering, she didn't know why she even existed. For a moment, she understood why Abby had attempted suicide years ago.

She hid her face in her hands and felt herself being manoeuvred out of her seat and outside, with a soft voice telling her that she would be all right, that she was safe and all she needed was to lay down for a few minutes.

When she next looked around, she couldn't remember how she had got here to the new surroundings. She registered the plush sofa under her in a light and airy living room and saw Lori in the armchair next to her.

Was she in Lori's home? She looked at her wristwatch. It was past three o'clock.

"I brought you to my place, I hope it's okay. I didn't think you'd want to go home yet, and... I gave you one of my Valium. Only a small dose."

Lori's concern was touching. "Thank you.... You're a Godsend." Rachel tried to stop her lips from trembling. "I'm so sorry, Lori."

"Don't mention it."

She tried to get up but felt a little wobbly. "Wow." She sat back down.

"Stay as long as you need. Or would you like me to call your husband for you? Or anyone else?"

Rachel shook her head. "No, he'll be home soon enough. And there's no one else. My sister's away, and my friend Tina's going through a rough time with... her divorce." Was she mumbling? She felt numb all over as tears cooled on her face. "I know my husband well and this news will devastate him. I can't tell him... Our marriage can't survive this... and I wouldn't blame—" Sobs racked her body as she felt Lori hold her tightly as if they were blood sisters.

"Oh, Rachel, I'm so sorry." She said gently. "I'm sorry for both of us."

∼

When JT's voice awoke her, she turned towards him in their semi-dark bedroom. "I'm sorry, honey, I'm not feeling well at all."

"What's the matter? What is it, Rachel?"

She had made him worried, darn it. "Nothing that a little sleep won't fix." Rachel tried to keep the tremble out of her voice. Taking in a deeper breath she said, "I've left your dinner in the fridge. Just reheat it..."

"Don't worry about... have you been crying, Rachel?"

"My nose is just stuffy and I'm sleepy."

"Is there anything I can get you?" He held her hand between his two, leaning to kiss her forehead.

"No, I'll just sleep it off...."

"Are you sure?"

"Yes, go and eat. I love you."

"I love you, too. Call me if you need anything." He kissed her again and quietly left the room.

∼

Something was amiss with Rachel and James felt helpless. Since the night three weeks ago when he had found her deeply asleep at seven in the evening, he almost didn't recognize his wife. He had been wrong in thinking that once Abby left for her own place he would have Rachel back to the way they used to spend time together.

But it wasn't just her.

His work days seemed to catch up with him and he felt drained by the time Friday evening rolled in. If he didn't force himself to keep his word to his brother, he would have cancelled their tennis or squash sessions. But he didn't. Waking up before the eight o'clock alarm bell on Saturday, he had hoped Rachel would still be asleep beside him. But like over the past weeks, he discovered that she was already out.

Getting ready for his squash game with Adam, James entered the kitchen. The lemony-pine scent filled the eerily quiet space. These days, Rachel seemed more interested in keeping the already gleaming house clean and running around for Tina and Abby. At first, he had been glad that helping at Abby's restaurant had kept Rachel too busy to fret about herself, but now something had shifted within her.

Was she patiently giving him his space, waiting for his workload to lighten? Or had his preoccupation finally pushed her away? They hadn't made love in ages. He missed her. Maybe in addition to it all, she hadn't ovulated in the past couple of months and was that why she wasn't mentioning anything about wanting a baby?

Poor Rachel. Where was she? And how could he reach her if she hardly talked to him?

He was losing her.

Reliving the day of the test results, Rachel couldn't understand JT's increasing broodiness. Or did he also instinctively know it was all futile?

For the past six weeks they had hardly spent any quality time together. She had still not told him about the results. Guilt charged through her. She was hurting them both. JT deserved better than an infertile and deceitful wife keeping the truth from him.

Their lives seemed to go in opposite directions. Unimaginable but true.

Rachel thanked God for the mercy of meeting Lori. She had been her true angel on that horrible day. Three days after the devastating test results, ignoring Brandon's silver-coloured card within her bag, she had scanned her mobile's contact list.

Calling Lori, she had thanked her again for helping her that day. Despite her own life-threatening situation, the beautiful soul had stayed with Rachel as if they were long lost sisters. Grandma Nancy had been right about the cliché of not judging a book by its cover. Looking at Lori, no one would have guessed that genetic heart issues and high blood pressure were endangering her life. She admired how Lori was still going ahead with her decision to have the baby, even if she couldn't—wouldn't—keep it.

"Despite your own news, you were so very kind for being there for me when I was in such shock. I really appreciate it. And... I wonder if you're available for coffee?"

Lori had seemed pleased to hear from her. "It's really good to hear from you, Rachel. I've been thinking about you and was going to call you in a couple of days. I've taken some time off to think through my... dilemma, so I'd love to get together for coffee... even today."

They met at the local coffee shop an hour later.

Over the past six weeks their frequent heart-to-hearts over coffee, lunch and their various Zumba and yoga classes were

Rachel's highlights of her otherwise miserable life in limbo. Living a lie and keeping secrets from her soul mate.

On one of their first outings, Rachel had picked up that living in such a close-knit community, Lori wouldn't divulge the impending father's identity. Not that it mattered to Rachel.

"You or your husband might know him, or his family, for God's sake." Lori had mock shuddered. Although she'd said it lightly, Rachel respected her new friend's request.

Since then, as if by silent mutual agreement, they talked about their work in general terms, like Lori's medical background while Rachel shared easily about her own working situation with Gareth. Lori referred to the obviously unavailable man who had got her pregnant as her 'five-minute mistake'. But she had shared openly about her regrets. "That's what happens when one lets ambition get in the way. What a fool I was... Driven to avenge my father was so stupid and immature. He's not who I thought he was, thanks to Mum's poisoning. She got Dad to marry her because she was pregnant and I'm no better than her or my so-called 'weak' Dad who fell in love with a younger woman, and left us for her."

"You're different from either of them. And you didn't know this guy was not single. Of *course* you didn't want to be alone after hearing about your dad's... heart attack." Lori had shared the full story of that one-night stand and Rachel admired how brave and selfless her friend was to be doing the right thing. Many women with her past would never risk their careers never mind their lives.

Seeing that faraway look on Lori's face she added, "How were you supposed to know that this guy was an opportunistic pig with his young bad-boy vibe?"

"When he got to my flat I suppose I just let myself feel and hope that it was more than just lust and loneliness. I can't even say the sex was even worth it." Lori's voice was low as she looked around the busy lunchtime crowd.

"Once you fall in love, really fall in love, you'll know it's worth it. Take it from this wise, old lady."

"I don't plan to ever fall in love." Lori grinned. "And at thirty-three, you're hardly old."

"Well, I feel old but still not wise." As they talked, Rachel resolved to help the young woman who reminded her so much of Abby.

Getting to know each other, it felt refreshing to have someone she could lean on rather than feel needed.

In turn, Lori took every opportunity between her work travels and other responsibilities to be with her. Rachel determined to take her words to heart. "You're here for me, too. It works both ways, Rachel. I've never known anyone I felt so open with. Or trusted so suddenly, so fast. You make me feel less alone."

Again, Rachel thanked God for meeting Lori. It helped her focus elsewhere, knowing now that their friendship meant equally as much to each other. She needed time to think all this through about the finality of the results as well as Dr. Carter's urging for surgery. Since the results, as if the shock had affected her body, her menstrual cycle was all screwed up, where her period came every ten or eleven days. Then her last one lasted almost ten days and at one point was so painful and debilitating that Rachel had to take a rare day off sick from work. Dr. Carter had warned her about the adenomyosis.

But she wouldn't have the hysterectomy yet.

Would JT leave her as soon as she told him the truth?

CHAPTER 28

Having returned yesterday from yet another trip to Wellsley Valley, Lauren updated James. He was relieved the news wasn't as dire as he had feared. "So there's still some ways to go, but I admit I'd expected more resistance. Well done, Lauren."

Discussing the various strategies for the next hour, he then saw Lauren's shoulders rise slightly, her eyes betraying her patent discomfort. "About what we'd discussed before I left... About me moving on. Now that we've both had time to think this through properly..." A small frown furrowed her forehead. "Once I start showing next month," she put a hand on her flat tummy, "people will talk, and because we've been working together so closely... Especially in Wellsley Valley... they may think it's...." She looked away for a moment and then added. "You know it'll cause issues even if I divulged who the father is. Which I won't."

"I already saw the ripples on the night of the gala. If you really need to leave, you can rest assured you'll have excellent references from us." James looked closely at her. "But as far as I'm concerned, I'd still like you to stay. The gossip will follow wherever you go."

She seemed more vulnerable, more real somehow. She nodded

and her expression made it clear that she was moved by his words.

Who else did she have? And placing her trust in him completely with her situation made him feel glad that he could somehow help. But how?

And Rachel would understand if he explained the whole situation to her. Surely, his wife knew she had his absolute devotion. His gut told him that Rachel would help this young woman if she only could.

And unlike many wives whose suspicions would have been roused after Dave's stunt at the gala, she had accepted his words of reassurance that everything was all right. Especially after trying to help her friend Tina to pick up the pieces of her life after marriage, Rachel was incredible. And his heart constricted at her justifiable impatience to get pregnant. He wished he could do more to help.

He sighed. "I wish you could meet my wife. She'd know how to help. She always knows. Always there for everyone." But he knew it would hurt Rachel too much. What could make her feel even more devastated, if not frustrated, than seeing a young woman who clearly didn't want the baby or any part of motherhood? "She's good in a crisis but right now…"

"You're excellent in a crisis, James. And it's so nice to see how much you love your wife. She must be very special. I've got this new friend who has been my lifeline. I don't know what I'd have done without you and her these past weeks. But I refuse to drag you down with me; you're too good a mentor."

She stood up and stared at him. "It's time for me to take responsibility for my own mistakes and I won't let your reputation be sullied or even questioned in any way."

As he started to shake his head she added, "Please, James, my instincts are hardly ever wrong. And I've considered the options of either transferring to America or accepting the position Parthenon offered me a couple of months ago."

"I appreciate you being so considerate on my behalf, but as I said, you know how small the Pharma industry is, and wherever you go, the gossip will follow." Again Rachel came to mind, and the way Dave's words had unsettled her. He would call her after this meeting and wouldn't take 'no' for an answer to take her out for dinner tonight.

They needed each other. He had to reach her before it was too late. And he would talk with her about Lauren and her situation and get her take on things.

He missed her in their bed since she'd moved to sleep in the guest room bed since she had caught a bad cold last week. He needed to speak with Rachel. And it would also ensure nothing else was left to chance or misunderstanding.

He waited for Lauren to respond and could see that she was making an effort to come to terms with the facts and that her pregnancy could not stay a secret.

She sighed and looked like a trapped bird. "I wish I was one of those people who could just ab.... get rid of the embryo and go on with my life."

He flinched and after a moment of silence asked, "So, you're absolutely sure that you won't keep the baby once you have it?"

"Yes, absolutely. Even my friend Rachel thinks I'd be a good mother, but she doesn't know me that well." Her cheeks flushed, and something deep inside him shook at the injustice of life. Of all the names in all the world why was Lauren's friend named Rachel? God certainly had a great sense of humor.

But James wasn't laughing.

"Let's focus on the positives and the options you have and I'll help in whichever way I can. But your contributions to the company make you indispensable."

With a sarcastic snort she said, "You and I both know no one's indispensable." As she looked into his eyes she added, "But, thank you. You don't know how much this means to me, James. You're a truly good man." She lowered her head but he saw her tears.

"Sorry, all the damned hormones are making me emotional and weepy." Her short laugh sounded like a sniff as she turned towards the door.

When she thanked him and left, the damned phone kept ringing and urgent emails kept pinging until it was too late to call Rachel. The five o'clock teleconference Mac had organized didn't end until past seven. He had to text Rachel and 'book' a romantic date over the coming weekend so she wouldn't get too busy again.

When had their lives become this crazy and disjointed?

CHAPTER 29

Perspiring hard, Rachel had loved every minute of the past hour's gruelling Zumba routine. She was glad she had listened to Lori and joined her even though she felt drained inside. Even though her now erratic and heavy periods were leaving her zapped of energy, exercise was good. And she enjoyed spending time with Lori whenever her friend was back in town.

Her days kept her occupied by overseeing the smooth running of Abby's café after she stayed in Israel for a couple of extra weeks. She missed her sister but was glad to get the Whatsapp updates with amazing photos of her vacation. Abby was fine, thank God.

Rachel also kept Tina and her boys as busy as she could. On the days when she was home alone even for short spurts, the silences were deafening. But when JT was at home, too, the tension and the emptiness within her reminded her again of her biggest failing.

These days, JT's martyr-like expression made her wonder if he somehow knew she could never give him a child. Was he that embroiled in his work that it took over most of the days including the weekends?

Or had he stopped loving her?

As excruciating as the possibility was, Rachel wished he would get it over and done with.

Bury the marriage so she could add that to her grieving process.

But neither broached the subject. Because she was the one keeping the results secret. And it was eating away at her. She cooked, cleaned, and slept in the spare room since using her bad cough and cold almost four weeks ago as an excuse not to keep JT up at night. Especially with the late nights he put in at work. When had it become a habit to sleep in separate parts of the house?

Despite his best intentions with his texts and phone calls, something always delayed him. She was trying to be patient while waiting for the right time to talk with him. But she couldn't.

～

Over the summer months Lauren had been seeing Rachel every available chance she got between her travels to Wellsley Valley and her increasingly busy work days. She didn't feel as guilty these days about keeping her work and position a secret from Rachel. Because the wonderful woman seemed to truly understand her need for discretion from the beginning. When she had explained to Rachel that she was in medicine and she travelled a lot it had been sufficient for her, and since then they referred to the men in their lives in broad terms. It was liberating to be able to talk to Rachel about everything.

Now, as her friend opened up her yoga mat beside her, she saw clearly that Rachel was still not interested in much, but was going through the motions of exercising because Lauren had asked her to keep her company. Sitting next to her in the large studio with more people arriving, she asked, "Are you all right? Have you spoken with your husband about..?"

"No. Still can't go through with it. I don't know what he'll do. He hardly seems to want to be in the same room as me."

Lauren was certain that his business was adding more strain on him. She couldn't remember what Rachel's husband did but it didn't matter. Running one's own company could burn a man out. Rachel had said that he also worked in central London, making Lauren wonder if she had ever taken the same train, or even compartment, from Oakwood station with him and never knew it.

"And I'm no better... hiding this huge secret."

Lauren saw the raw pain in her eyes, before Rachel lowered her head, resting her hands on her legs in their lotus position. She seemed jumpy and on edge at the smallest sounds around them.

"How can I help you, Rachel?"

"No one can help me but myself."

It was an alien feeling to care for someone and to feel such trust and deep affection so easily. Since her great-aunt's passing, the only person Lauren had cared about was Lauren. It hurt to see that Rachel was not only a wonderful woman but she would be a perfect mother. Since losing her father to another woman and her mother to alcohol abuse, Lauren wasn't surprised at life's cruel twists. What *did* surprise her though was the kindness of the two people in her life right now, who made her feel loved and cared for. As if she deserved their kindness.

"I'd know what to do, I'm just a coward... I don't know how to broach the subject or start the conversation. And you should have heard my mother-in-law on the phone yesterday. She had the gall to call me at work and ask me if I'd considered IVF as her son deserved to be a father sooner rather than later."

Lauren gasped and shook her head. "So you never told them that DH's sperm count was low?" Lori's distancing nickname for 'dear husband' made it easier for them to openly discuss whatever was on their minds.

"No, why would I have had to? But it's all a moot point now."

Rachel groaned and as Lauren gripped her friend's hand, she could tell she was forcing herself to stop crying, "I'm falling apart and making it all about me again, I'm sorry. You've got such a big decision to make... your own life complications..."

"In a way, it helps me to take the focus off myself. So, again, selfishness on my part."

From Rachel's frank look, Lauren saw she wasn't convinced.

"You're one special person, Lori. And I have a strong feeling that you'll be a great mother. And if you let me, I'll be with you every step of the way. You'll see, you'll love it the moment you'll set eyes on it."

Only Lauren knew herself so much better than this generous, romantic woman who deserved to have her dreams come true.

"Maybe that's why we met when we did. I don't ever want you to feel alone again."

For the first time in weeks, Lauren saw a glint of something in her friend's eyes. And shook her head. "You're too generous. You have too much faith and when you get to know me better... you'll be disappointed in me."

"I don't think so. In fact, I know you can never disappoint me. But more importantly, you have to see how amazing and brave you are. Just think about what I said. Okay?"

Then the class started and Lauren wasn't in the mood for yoga and contemplation anymore.

Because despite her friend's faith and not wanting to disappoint Rachel or her kind boss, James, one thing was for sure: Lauren would never keep this baby.

CHAPTER 30

"So how's DH?" Despite Lori's casual question, Rachel knew what her friend was asking as they sat in one of their favorite local restaurants in Oakwood, on this beautiful summer day. Had she grown a backbone and finally talked with JT?

After the busiest yet longest summer in her life, Rachel still hadn't. Couldn't.

"He's the same." She sighed, no nearer a breakthrough. Sick and tired of thinking and convoluting about it. "I can't wait for you to meet Abby. She's coming back next week. She's very smart and artistic."

"Okay, change of subject noted." Lori smiled at her. "We've talked about her so much I feel like I know Abby already. Do you know if she's over that guy?"

"I think so. I hope so, and her therapist sounds great. I'm proud that she's gone for help. Maybe I should go and see him myself." She half joked.

Lori studied her. "It may help with your limbo, as you call it."

"You remind me of Abby. She's so deep, so loving and yet so misunderstood."

Lori laughed, surprise written on her face. That chesty, joyful sound always made Rachel happier.

"But you're stronger than she is, more resilient." Lori's confidence and joy for life resonated from her, despite her own predicament. Rachel could tell how some scents around them made her friend feel queasy, but admired how she handled it with grace, not mentioning it or complaining.

"So you think I'm misunderstood, do you?"

"Well..." She smiled. "Didn't you say that your family... your Dad doesn't really get you?"

Lori nodded and shrugged, but from the stories she had shared, Rachel knew that it still hurt her a lot.

"You've gone through so much that you've learned to cover up your inner emotions so you don't get hurt anymore. And I know you're very kind and loving. Look at what you've done for your twin brothers."

Over the past few months Lori had slowly and cautiously reconnected with them.

"Half-brothers."

"You saved those boys from getting sucked deeper into that cult. I still can't believe how you managed to do all that research and investigation, expose the crooks and still stay anonymous. Your father and step-mother would be so glad to thank you if they knew you were behind it all."

"I merely saw options others—including my dear father and step-mother—couldn't see. No big deal." She had the right contacts high up in the legal world and it showed Rachel how respected her friend was to have discreet help on such a high-profile level.

Rachel shook her head at how Lori underplayed her role and her help. "I'm proud of you, if that doesn't sound condescending." Rachel then added, "and from that proud twinkle in your eyes I know you love your brothers."

Lori rolled her eyes and grinned. Rachel knew that 'I know

what I want and I'm going to get it' look made men run for cover. Yet Lori seemed unaware of her own charm and beauty. Or at least didn't seem to use it to advance herself in her career from what she had learned about her over the past few months.

"If you hadn't talked me into going to see my father I wouldn't be the hero you make me out to be."

Only a couple of months ago, Rachel had felt so sad to hear about Lori's estranged relationship with her father. Lori had explained that even though she had always been invited to the various festivities, and they would have been polite to her, she knew she would always feel like the poor relation. Rachel knew from the woman she had got to know so well that Lori would never allow anyone to make her feel like a charity case.

"But the boys are something else." Her pride came through loud and clear, making Rachel smile again.

"You're downplaying how good it makes you feel. It's easier that way, isn't it? But you're no longer that little girl. You seeing them now is *your* own choice. And I'm glad. And I'm certain they're very proud of who you've become. We all need family."

Lori smiled and blushed. "Your sister's so lucky to have you." Then added, "I didn't realize how alone I've been all these years."

"You don't have to keep everyone at a distance."

"I'm not anymore. I can blame you for that, too. You're making me an emotional puddle."

"And it's nothing to do with your hormones." Rachel smiled back.

"I'll be really glad to have my own body back as soon as—" Lori stopped, her face stricken. "I've a lot to learn still about sensitivity to those around me."

"I get it. I do. Don't worry, Lori."

Rachel had never imagined being so comfortable and open with a girlfriend whose personality was so different from her own. And deep inside, she knew that Lori was capable of being a loving wife and mother and that it was pure fear that kept her believing in her self-sufficient independence. Every time they met, she learned something new about Lori's hard childhood and admired how she had turned her life around.

Time would tell about how she could help Lori. In the meantime, she would soldier on helping the absent Abby with the café and hoping something changed at home.

But nothing could change without her initiating it.

CHAPTER 31

As they sat having their quinoa salads and shared a veggie burger at a new organic restaurant in Cockfosters, Rachel could tell what was on Lori's mind on this overcast, humid August day.

"So have you told DH about the results, or talked to him about other options?"

"No." Her voice sounded whiny. "By now you've realized what a big coward I am." She sighed, pushing away the pain that instantly lay on her chest at the reasonable question. "I don't know how he'll react. The words won't come."

"You must love him a lot. Or you wouldn't still be trying to find a way."

"But I don't think he loves *me*. I don't know why he won't admit it if he's no longer... We're like those old couples after fifty years together, too tired to communicate, never mind think about starting over again... I wish I had half your courage and your calm, making such a life changing—and life threatening—decision about having the baby and..." She couldn't voice the words 'giving it up for adoption'.

Giving away a part of herself.

At least Lori was being open and truthful with herself. Rachel on the other hand was living—or existing in limbo, in a lie.

The heaviness within her chest grew. She tried to push through the constant pain within her heart and her abdomen. Which seemed always; even during the night when she awoke in tears, alone, or when the alarm bullied her into another empty day.

"I don't know how you do it, but I'm so glad that you accept me the way you do. You're very caring... always thinking about others. And always there for me."

"You could also interpret it that maybe it's easier not to think about my own problems, so I meddle with other people's lives."

"You don't meddle."

"Oh, no, and I don't nag either." Rachel arched an eyebrow at how she had pushed away her once adoring husband.

"I believe it's genuine caring. I've never had a girlfriend—a best friend," Lori's smile was so sweet it made Rachel smile. "To really talk with and to be so open about everything. I can't believe how you're not judgemental about this," she pointed to her protruding stomach under the loose folds of the flowing summer dress. "That takes a lot of sincerity and strength from someone who's going through what you're going through."

"There were times I used to envy my friends, all of them were either going through morning sickness, breastfeeding or getting married to get pregnant—you know the race to beat the body clock."

Lori put her hand on Rachel's. "It must be so hard..."

"And there I was, feeling lousy, selfish and mean-spirited towards people I've known for years...instead of being happy for them."

"And here you are now, befriending a wanton woman whose five minutes of sex lands her in this mess. No lover, no room in her life for a baby."

"Are you sure the father wouldn't...?"

"I'm sure. And I want nothing to do with him. And I'm getting legal advice to ensure he doesn't have any contact with the baby if he later changes his mind. All I know for sure is that it shouldn't have happened, but it did. And it's my responsibility, no one else's."

"I don't know if it's my imagination..." Some small alarm reverberated from deep within her. "Maybe I'm being paranoid, I feel he's... there's someone else. That I've lost him and I can't face asking him, telling him the truth...." She tried to breathe in but the constricted airways seemed even tighter as she pushed away the burning tears from behind her eyelids.

"From what you've told me, I can't believe that. You suspect his work is really tough right now. You've run your own business, surely you can understand what pressure can do to you."

"I'd love to blame his workaholic tendencies, but... in my gut I know he's no longer in love with me. Since I met Brandon again and when we went out for lunch he made me feel special and desirable... I should either jump JT and leave him no choice... Or maybe I should just have a bloody affair myself." Rachel's comical attempt fell flat as soon as the words were out of her mouth.

CHAPTER 32

*L*ori's astute eyes stayed steady on Rachel's face, making her flush.

"You know an affair is no joking matter. Take it from someone who was at the other end of one and repeating the pattern. You'd have thought I'd know better after seeing my parents make a bloody mess of their marriage. Instead, this, for God's sake," again she touched her belly. "With every day I'm realizing my similarities with Mum."

"You're nothing like her." Rachel was flabbergasted. "Your Mum had got your father to marry her because she was pregnant, and here you are completely independent, and opting to do all this on your own."

"Why was I even attracted to the guy.... a weak selfish man who obviously doesn't give a fig about his marital vows?"

"You're being too hard on yourself, Lori. Life's messy and no one has the perfect answers."

"I'd have thought my past would have taught me that much. And I trusted the first guy who showed an interest in me."

"I'm sure there are many men who'd love to get to know you." Rachel took it for granted. "But more to the point, look at how strong you are, and you're doing such an amazing thing, having the baby, despite the danger to your own life."

Lori may have told her that she would never contemplate keeping the baby, but Rachel held hope within her heart for her friend. After hearing about Lori's family history of heart issues and high blood pressure, Rachel further admired the strength within her friend and the capacity to love unconditionally.

She hoped that her own yearnings to hold a baby against her own bosom didn't come through. Instead, she prayed for time to heal and help Lori make her decision without her past overshadowing everything else.

"We're both risking our lives, but I won't lose you. Some women are Mother Nature themselves. Like I could easily imagine you—sorry, Rachel, you know what I mean..." Lori picked up her cup of herbal tea.

"I'm just refusing to face reality or talk to my husband." She bit the inside corner of her lower lip staring down at her cappuccino.

As if aware that her friend was on the brink of tears, Lori said, "Because you love him so much. I've never been exposed to that kind of caring... well, apart from now with Dad and Marilyn.

"I can't understand women like your mother, and my own."

"Mine was an alcoholic, and violent with it." Lori sighed and thankfully allowed her to stop thinking about herself for a while.

"I was seven when my mother drove us to Dad's new house...everything changed after that day... It was actually my seventh birthday and Mum dragged me outside this big house. Dad had been 'away at work' more and more frequently and I was missing him. But when this young woman opened the door and my father came to stand behind her, I was confused." Lori took in a slow breath and continued. "Then this cute little puppy started running around their feet and jumped out towards me. It rushed to me and smelled my hand... I loved it so much. It was so soft and fun and... Then I heard Mum asking him to come home, and she started to scream at them. Something about how could he leave his own family and how could he miss his own daughter's seventh birthday? And when my Dad came towards her she wouldn't let him, shouting that he was a philanderer, and that he'd never see me again as long as he lived. Unless he gave up his whore." Lori sighed. "He kept saying that he was sorry, and that he loved me. That made her even angrier. He begged Mum to let me move in with them, saying he'd give me a better life than what she could offer.

"Even at that age, I saw that nothing would be the same again. Even as she drove us home saying that she loved me more than anything in the world, Mum had no time for me after that day. She became cold and bitter, escaping into alcoholic oblivion. In one of her rages, when she was awake, she blamed me for all her troubles, for giving up her ballet career because she'd got pregnant with me. That she had never wanted me. I used to think she was so beautiful, so petite and elegant. She had pictures of herself as a ballerina all over the house. But as a teen I suddenly saw how self-centered she was."

Rachel watched Lori's faraway expression, the lower lip quivering slightly as she continued. Was she talking about this for the first time in her life? As if the unplanned life within her was forcing her to face scarring past wounds.

"She'd shun me and then she'd slag off Dad to me, maligning him for not loving her, for leaving us. I'd watched her wither into a shell, having convinced herself she was worthless. That she was nothing without the man to whom she'd devoted herself. She was twenty-seven when he left, for God's sake. She should have stopped drinking Vodka like it was water, and gotten on with her life." That cold glare made Rachel's own blood boil, wishing she could console her somehow. All she could do was listen.

"If I didn't prepare something to eat we'd have both starved. By the time I was twelve, I knew how to roast a chicken and make really good crunchy potatoes." Her cynical smile disappeared when she added, "If there was nothing left in the kitchen I'd try and wake her while she lay unconscious on the sofa. Giving up, I'd take some cash out of her bag—if there was any—and get some fast food downstairs. Some people have no right to be parents."

Rachel hugged Lori into herself, until her friend's head rested on her shoulder. She stayed silent, somehow divining that Lori needed to share all this out loud.

At almost three in the afternoon, their quiet surroundings made it easier to talk. Rachel motioned for their server for another cappuccino and hot water.

"I had to clean up the house and bathe Mum's inevitable gashes when she'd fall off the sofa or down the stairs. Once she cut her head on the corner of the coffee table and needed five stitches. I was terrified the hospital would take her away from me. I'd wondered what would happen to me if she... if something horrible happened to her. Can you believe I grew up needing her so much, that I believed if I loved her as much as I could I'd make it all better?"

"But it never got better." Rachel shook her head.

Lori's hand shook slightly as she poured hot water from her little pot into her nearly empty cup.

"After we're done here, do you want to take a long walk around the park?"

Lori nodded, and later Rachel paid for them both and they drove to the local park where they loved spending hours walking. The heat of the day was calming, and Rachel watched Lori's downcast eyes, "On many days I returned from school and was at the receiving end of Mum's rages and I'd hear her whimpering into her pillows at night. I kept asking God—I used to believe in him in those foolish days—what the hell was life all about?"

"How old were you when she...?"

"I was fourteen when her liver gave up on her. She kept right on drinking until her last dying breath." Lori said this as if she was spent now. All hardness had left her voice and her features as they settled into a shaded bench.

"No way was I going to live with Dad, and almost all Mum's relatives refused to have me, 'the carrot-topped fat teen with attitude' I'd overheard my uncle call me. None of them liked me because I resembled my Dad. I have his eyes and his hair. Great legacy, ha? Great joke."

"I think you're gorgeous." Rachel said. "It's like you take it for granted. Abby has silky straight hair, but she dyes it dark brown, almost black. I think she doesn't want to look like our Mum did. Isn't it creepy how our mums seemed to have so many similar self-destructive tendencies? Anyway, go on, that's when you moved in with your great-aunt Agnes?"

Lori nodded. "She was lovely. Despite her old age and arthritis, she was so kind and loving. A lot like you." Lori's smile was sweet, as if the memory warmed her, making her believe in hope and possibilities of what *could* be. "She was the only one who used to call me Lori, not Lauren. Anyway, she kept trying to explain about the truth behind Mum and Dad's relationship from years back. But, as stubborn as usual, I didn't trust him, his wife or even the twin boys. I suppose I was jealous."

"I get that. I would be too."

"I really thought they were all pretending, that underneath they were all miserable. Wasn't everyone?" There was a long silence.

"You make my own childhood seem almost normal the way you had to look after yourself and your mother."

"That's what alcoholism can do. And I hardly ever drink because I'd promised myself never to start, so I'd never get hooked." Lori shrugged. "And I suspect that there's a lot more in your own childhood that is probably hard for you to think about."

"You're a very smart young woman, Lori." She knew she was trying to push away at the truth of her friend's astute remark. "But just because your mother didn't want... children doesn't mean that you won't be a great—" Rachel nodded towards Lori's stomach.

"You still don't know me..." Lori took in a deep breath and let it out as they started on another long route around the increasingly busy park. "The truth is that after moving in with Aunt Agnes, even if she didn't make me feel like a burden, I promised myself that I'd never be responsible for another human being other than myself. It was less complicated all around."

"It hurt less." Rachel understood that. "But you were a young teenager, Lori, now you're an adult." Rachel understood that especially in her vulnerable state, Lori's defence mechanism was her way of handling her past and her current 'unfortunate' situation. "And despite your insistence to the contrary, this experience is bringing out your caring side."

"No, that's on you." Lori's eyes twinkled in gratitude.

"What if you feel differently once you see your baby?" The lump in her throat hurt. "Just don't make any decisions you may regret later."

"I know myself. And I also get how you'd think all women would feel that way." Lori touched her hand. "You're such a special person and so non-judgmental, I can't believe my luck in meeting you."

Rachel respected her friend's honesty. Everyone made mistakes, so why would she judge Lori for hers?

She may have said she didn't care to have any part of romance, marriage or children—while it was Rachel's whole life—but Lori was so warm and kind that it was obvious she would be a good mother. And Rachel would help her see that over the next few months while the... foetus grew within her womb.

Wasn't this why they had met?

CHAPTER 33

"Are you okay, Raych?" Abby asked Rachel who seemed extra pale. Or was it the airport's grey concrete surroundings?

"I'm fine, thanks." Her sister smiled at her as they finally reached her Audi in Heathrow's congested car park.

"Thanks for picking me up, I appreciate it. And thanks again for running the café so well... Kevin's been singing your praises on Whatsapp and I feel quite redundant."

"You're welcome. How was it? Was it fun?" Rachel seemed distracted and didn't seem to be really listening. But her poor sister had enough on her plate. Abby would make it easier for her.

She sighed. "It was wonderful." She told her about her escapades starting from on board the schooner-cum-hotel she'd stayed in when first arriving in Eilat, glossing over the horrible incident that had her running for her life. And instead elaborated on how she got to know the real Israeli people in the last six weeks. "I met this artist, Avner, and before you think, 'there she goes again, falling in love willy-nilly', this was quite different. He's gorgeous, yes, but we got to know each other on a completely different level, you know? Just like Karl had coached me. Get to know the guys as friends, giving each other time to explore myself and what I'm really all about. And I started painting again, in his studio. It was like fate meeting such an artistic soul while getting ready to use the new studio space as soon as I got back here. He's just brilliant. I'm taking Avner's advice and getting back to it properly. I can do it. I've got the space and the talent. I can't wait. I'll just have to make some time for it. My therapist did say art could be a real salvation."

"I'm so excited for you. That's wonderful, Abs. So what happened with this... Avner? Is he coming here, are you going there again?"

Rachel glanced at her for a moment and Abby swallowed down her instant sadness at the perfectly reasonable question. "I made up my mind that it was best to leave it as it was: perfect. I know you'll say something about me getting cold feet or something..." She sighed again, "I miss him already, but it's best this way...."

Seconds ticked while Rachel was silent, distant.

"Earth to Rachel!"

Her sister snapped to attention. "Sorry, Abs, I was just concentrating on the traffic. Go on."

"Is everything all right? You don't seem..." Abby said hesitantly. "I can tell you've got a lot on your mind. It wasn't too much for you with the restaurant, was it?"

"No, of course not. Honestly, don't worry. Everything will work out. So tell me more about Avner. He sounds lovely."

Abby knew her sister well. Preferring not to dwell on her own issues, she always tried to help others. Almost like she always had to be the mother figure when their age gap was only eight years apart. Poor, lovely Rachel who deserved to be a mother of many children. "I finally know what really falling in love feels like. The way I see the bond and connection between you and James."

Had Rachel just made a snorting sound as they wrestled their way through the jammed M25? She studied her sister but couldn't be sure. But she wouldn't push her. "And I'm ready to go deeper with therapy and have hypnosis."

Abby noticed Rachel's frown.

"While I was away I've done some deep soul-searching. Karl has been asking questions about Mum and Dad. First I couldn't understand why he kept going on and on about them, I kept pushing it away. But he's explained that we need to look into the past to see what's stopping me from going forward in my life."

"Sounds practical. So is this coming out under hypnosis then?" She could tell that her sister seemed uncomfortable with the idea.

"Well, no. I've been afraid, I don't know why. But the nightmares had started again before I left for Israel."

"Oh, Abs." Rachel put her hand on hers for a moment.

"Do you want to move back in with us instead of being alone in the flat."

"If you're worried about me calling Rick..." Abby tried not to sound defensive.

"No, I thought you could come back for a few weeks, till maybe the therapy will bring stuff out."

Abby shook her head, "I think I'll be okay, but I'm still scared about being put under hypnosis, and I was wondering if you'd do me a favour."

"Anything, you know that."

"Karl said that if you could come in and talk to him, as you were older, he thinks you may shed some light on what happened back then."

"But that sounds a bit strange. Is it even ethical for me to see him? My views of what happened are quite different from what you experienced."

Abby felt a contraction of pain around her midriff, as if about to take a test, knowing she would fail, miserably. "I just don't know what else to do. I just have to do it." Abby took in a strained breath and then let it out, her shoulders hunching.

"I'll come and see him, just tell me where and when, I'll work around it."

"I really appreciate it. Thanks, sis." Abby smiled tightly. "I'll try it one more time. But knowing you're there for me, as usual, it means everything.

Despite her fears, somehow she felt her earlier excitement and hope rise, "I have so much to live for, my art, a wonderful sister who picks me up from the airport..." Her light-hearted words brought no reaction from Rachel. "And the restaurant... and absolutely no men. Thanks to Avner. I can't wait to speak to Karl."

Finally, Rachel glanced at her before focusing back on the road. "Are you sure about hypnosis? I've heard some things about false memories that can be instilled in patients' brains. Does this therapist know what he's doing?"

"Yes, absolutely."

Was that relief or was Rachel trying to take deeper breaths? "Obviously you've had one heck of a holiday, from your tan and the sparks flying from you." Rachel smiled with a warmth Abby felt was genuine, and that her sister was trying hard to be more present as they edged forward a little more through the traffic.

"The test results, they weren't good, were they? That's why I didn't hear from you?"

She watched Rachel try to compose words but nothing but a nod came.

"I'm so sorry, Raych," Abby gently touched her sister's tense shoulder. "I know you like to take care of everyone else, and you're the older sister, but please, Raych, let me help in whichever way I can. I'm here for you. I won't let you feel alone anymore."

From her slight tremble on her lower lip before she sat upright, Rachel squeezed her sister's hand. "I know, thank you, Abs. But there's nothing anyone can do. But I really appreciate it. I'm glad you're back."

"I'm serious. I'm nearly twenty-six and I'll prove to you that I'm finally growing up, and have turned a new chapter in my life. You've brought me up telling me there's always something that can be done." She waited almost holding her breath.

"I c—can't have children." Had Rachel forced herself to say it quickly?

"Oh, no." Abby squeezed Rachel's upper arm trying to quell her own deep sadness and disappointment knowing how it was devastating her sister, and there she was having a time of her life in the sun. "What are your options?" She asked quietly.

"I don't know. Not much."

Abby saw tears leak down her sister's face.

"And I've pushed poor JT too far with my obsession... And now..."

When she didn't seem capable of more words, Abby said, "Well, that's natural, isn't it? You've been doing everything possible. But surely he's very understanding."

"I don't want to burden you, but..." As Rachel inhaled and let a breath go, Abby's heart pounded as her sister added, "I haven't told him yet about the results."

Oh, God, things were much worse than she had imagined between James and Rachel.

"I think he's fallen out of love with me. After the gala, I even wondered if he's been having an affair."

"What? JT? No way!" Abby almost shrieked. "What makes you think that?"

"You've seen him when you stayed over. Now imagine no communication whatsoever between us." She added heatedly, wiping tears with a quick impatient forefinger under each eye.

She sniffed and grabbed a tissue from the car door alcove as if regretting saying anything.

"I'm sure you're wrong. I think he loves you so much..." After a pause she asked, "Surely it's his work and the redundancies?"

Rachel shook her head slowly.

No, not her sister's wonderful marriage, too! James and her sister seemed perfect for each other. Had he turned out as weak and animalistic as the rest? Her brother-in-law was insular and took time to open up to those around him, but he was one of the most devoted husbands she could have imagined for Rachel. He looked as if he truly adored her, loving her just as she was. Which was amazingly generous, loyal, strong and always positive.

They had seemed so happy and fulfilled together. But she *was* a romantic and idealist sometimes.

See the facts as they are, damn it.

She had been absolutely right to see her relationship with Avner for what it was. A platonic holiday, a beautifully liberating and rejuvenating summer fling, which had fully reawakened her artistic passions.

Goodbye. It was better, safer this way.

She wasn't sure what was causing the tightness in her chest once more; the inevitability of all relationships turning sour eventually, or that the memory of seeing Avner only days before, made her feel like a weakling for wishing she was still with him.

Her poor sister needed her and she was incapable of thinking about anyone but herself. She was such a loser. Her own tears seemed to threaten so she took more deep calming breaths and stayed in the moment like Karl had taught her.

But it wasn't quite working.

After long minutes she asked, "What are you going to do? My therapist would say you have to talk to JT."

Rachel sighed. "I know, I've been thinking the same thing. Don't worry. I'll get it all sorted. Now stop worrying about your spoilt sister's silly problems." Rachel's chin jutted out bravely as she manoeuvred the car around the corner from the café and her new flat.

Abby wished there was something she could do to help her suffering sister.

"There's a new friend of mine I'd like you to meet, Abs."

Rachel's smile warmed. "Lori is such a lovely person. I'm sure you'll really like each other."

As she heard about the 'amazing' pregnant young woman, something balled inside her.

CHAPTER 34

AUGUST

*O*ut of breath, Lauren was glad to have expended the energy in yet another fast-paced Zumba class. At over twenty-one weeks pregnant, she could hardly recognize her body when she caught a look in the bathroom mirror this morning. To add to her large breasts and protruding tummy, her bottom and upper thighs were starting to look too rounded and bulky, thanks to all her eating and crazy cravings.

Any scent of male cologne made her almost gag, sometimes needing to run to the bathroom, but at least her food stayed down now.

With another seventeen long weeks to go, she knew it would only get worse and she would grow in girth and weight. The headaches were starting to add to her sense of being taken over by an alien. Her blood pressure wasn't very good, but she kept to her regime and did everything the specialist told her to.

Soon, she would not be able to see her own feet or put on

shoes. Welcome to the world of sumo wrestlers. She gritted her teeth.

She turned and smiled at the huffing hot-faced Rachel beside her. Lauren had noticed her brave friend's low stamina and frequent water breaks over the session and how she was increasingly getting slower over the past weeks. Lauren suspected that the adenomyosis the doctor had warned Rachel would become worse was now causing her more pain and, she suspected, increased bleeding.

"How are you doing?" She asked casually. "Are the iron tablets helping you?"

Rachel shrugged, shook her head and then nodded, "I'm fine. That was fun." Then added, "Now don't make me regret telling you about my constant... periods and about the doctor's warning."

"So it's worse... I'm sorry, I don't mean to nag but you know you can share anything with me."

"I know, I trust you completely." Although she smiled and hugged her, Lauren could see how the adenomyosis was affecting her. Dr. Carter was pushing Rachel to have the hysterectomy, but she was adamant she needed time to think about it.

"So you saw the acupuncturist? Did Lena help you?"

Okay, she was changing the subject again. Lauren sighed and nodded. "She's amazing. You were right. Who knew acupuncture could help with morning sickness and other stuff to make me feel more human?" Lauren wiped her face with her small towel as they left the sun-filled warm studio. "So she said you haven't seen her for a few weeks. Maybe she can help with the heavy periods."

They both knew it was much more than that.

"What's the use? Anyway, let's talk about something more interesting. How about doing lunch at Abby's café after this? You have the time?"

"I do. But I thought it's her birthday weekend. And what about your hubby?" It was Sunday and she felt conscious that Rachel was avoiding going home, yet again.

"He's not interes—around, so let's have nice girl time together. Abby invited us to a friend's art exhibition later, too. She celebrated her birthday with her other group and I took her out on Friday. I can't wait for you two to meet. And then we can have drinks and pizza at her place. You game?"

Rachel's bright smile didn't fool her, but she nodded. "Let's do it."

After the forty minute drive through the A10 and London's traffic, Rachel parked close enough to the restaurant and they settled in one of the small tables towards the back of Café Vert.

She adored their time spent together. Her flat seemed empty and uninviting and Rachel appreciated the distraction of being out, too. Work was getting busier and crazier at Wellsley Valley, but she knew her contributions were valued and that considering they were dealing with pig-headed employees who reviled change, her team alongside her were keeping everything in control. She was very conscious how much the increasing pressure of the merger was pushing James to his limits. She would do everything to help the company, and especially her mentor and friend.

Pushing aside her thoughts of work until tomorrow morning, she admired how the café's open windows to the quiet courtyard brought in a welcome end of summer breeze. She sighed, grateful not to feel nausea at any scents of food or perfume around her.

Like a miracle, as soon as she entered her fifth month of pregnancy, her constant queasiness abated. Instead, her appetite and crazy cravings took over. The obsessive hunger for strange combinations of food made her hungry even just thinking about them. Like potato wedges dunked in gravy and mint chocolate ice-cream or sucking on large halves of fresh lemon, and crunching lots of pickles in front of the TV. But she tried to keep all her developments low-key for Rachel's sake. She may not be happy about being the carrier of an unwanted foetus but she knew it must be hell for her friend on a different level.

Lauren knew she could never have been this generous and understanding if the roles had been reversed.

From the way the gorgeous young woman with long, almost-black hair strode towards them, Lauren was sure it was Rachel's sister. Abby greeted them, hugged her sister warmly and welcomed Lauren to the café. Lauren felt Abby's reserved coolness towards her through her professionalism and valiant attempt at being hospitable. Rachel seemed oblivious to this, but Lauren could handle it. After all, she knew nothing about the imposter who was spending so much time with her older sister.

"I hear you're an artist, I look forward to seeing your pieces whenever you're ready." She was giving her an out for their later plans that Rachel had mentioned for this evening.

After a pause, Abby nodded and smiled, "It's no big deal. Rachel and I are having a quiet evening in after the exhibition. You're welcome to join us, if you'd like." The message in her dark wide blue eyes was clear.

Lauren was the outsider. But Abby had been taught manners by her older sister.

Not to add any more pressure on Rachel, Lauren nodded and said, "Let's see how the show goes and if I'm not too tired after that."

Rachel said, "I mentioned your pregnancy to Abby. I was sure it would be okay with you."

"Of course. I'm already looking and feeling big. Although I can see that some people aren't sure if I've just put on a lot of weight. But they'll all know soon enough despite my baggy outfits." She tried to smile to keep it light as she smoothed down her oversize tunic and trendy long cardigan over her comfy black elastic-waisted leggings.

This morning, she was disappointed that already she couldn't fit into her boots.

Why did women do this to themselves voluntarily, sometimes more than once?

As Abby made small talk with them, a loud crash reverberated from the direction of the kitchen.

Lauren saw the exotic beauty wince without moving a muscle. Abby's long hair framing her delicate face didn't hide how she willed herself to stay calm. "There she goes again." She sighed and looked heaven-wards. "I'll come and keep you company later." She looked at Lauren. "That's our Nadia, the manager's aunt. One of the 'helpers'. Hm!" She rolled her eyes and smiled. Her voice somewhat quieter she added, "Her arthritic fingers are dropping more dishes than her wages could afford but what the heck can I do? No one will hire her."

"You're caring and that's not a bad trait, Abs. So go on. We'll be here. Visit us whenever you have time... if you have time." Rachel smiled and on cue, a shattered glass from somewhere close took Abby away. "Excuse me. Enjoy, both of you."

The edginess in those blue eyes betrayed that Abby was far from calm or content as she ran the restaurant like a well-oiled machine. The way her eyes scanned the front doors and windows made Lauren wonder if she still feared seeing Rick.

"She's so soft-hearted, like you are, and covers it up well, just like you." Rachel grinned, obviously relaxing at the temporary distraction from her own issues. Yet again, she dreaded asking if Rachel had broached the subject with her husband. And knew that she hadn't. Lauren would have heard about it immediately. She tried not to nag or push but knew that with every week that passed, the marriage could be lost forever. And more frightening, the delay of having the surgery could be fatal to Rachel.

CHAPTER 35

The food at the café was excellent and the atmosphere hip and hectic. Lauren was relieved that her chosen dish of avocado salad with the poppy-seed dressing on the side was staying down.

After Nadia had gingerly taken away their empty lunch plates, Lauren glanced at Rachel and again broached the subject that was troubling her.

"I know you don't want to hear this but I'm worried about you. And I wish there was some other way, but you *have* to make the appointment for the surgery. I can see that you're pale and tired. I'm afraid to lose the only best friend I have... I'll be there with you, and you must trust your husband. Talk to him. This is gone on for... nearly three months now. It's crazy."

"You don't know how close we were, Lori. And I can't believe it myself."

"What if you're underestimating him?"

Rachel put down her fork on the edge of her bowl of quinoa salad with sprouted beans. "Thank you, I appreciate it... but I can't face the finality of it. And what if he's fallen out of love with me? What if he *is* having an affair and I'm just convincing myself that it's his work?" She shook her head. "What if he admits that... and again I force his hand... and he leaves?

Dread penetrated through Lauren and she shook her head, "No. I won't believe that. You have to bite the bullet and face him with your suspicions. Because you can't go on like this, either way. From what you've told me about your marriage until these past couple of months... he sounds like a really... loving man."

"I know but I can't..." Rachel added with a sad smile, "If I hadn't seen the horror an affair can cause from Tina's situation I'd have probably..."

Lauren sat up, "You're not thinking about seeing Brandon, are you?"

"No. But he is—was—the only man who seems interested in me." The momentary spark from Rachel's wan face was gone.

It must be terrible to need someone else's approval to feel important or valuable.

But wasn't she herself depending on James and this wonderful woman?

After their many talks together, mainly at her flat or anywhere other than Rachel's house, she realized that her friend hated being at home alone. Lauren thanked her lucky stars at how accepting and non-judgmental Rachel was. So she had no problem in voicing her fears.

Yes, her heart went out to Rachel but she had seen first-hand how infidelity damaged many lives. Protecting from any hurt was far better all around than having to deal with life-changing consequences. Just as she was taking no risks from any ripple effects of her own mistakes. She had insisted that Vincent, the father of the child she was carrying, sign legal documents to guarantee that he would never have any contact with her or the baby.

"You can trust me with anything you tell me, and I may be pot calling the kettle black, but I hope you're not serious about this ex. Although now that I've got to know you better, and I don't think you're the type to do it, no matter what you're thinking right now..." Lauren paused for a moment, and added gently, "We both know it wouldn't solve anything. Right?"

Rachel nodded and sighed. "Of course, I know. I've got enough going on in my life right now without... And I've told Brandon I'm not interested. He's dealing with Gareth from now on, and I'm not sure I can go on working there."

"You mean you've been working with this Brandon?" At Rachel's nod she sucked her breath in and let it out. This made sense now. Rachel was spending time with this guy during their work days, getting closer to each other while DH was probably working his tail off and not interested in anything but sleep at the end of the day. "Inevitably someone always gets hurt and there are all sorts of consequences. I'm talking from experience." Lauren touched her hard, rounded belly.

"Don't worry, Lori, I know." Rachel's smile made her relax. "It's so nice to feel so cared for. Thanks."

"Ditto." Lauren couldn't help but add, "And spending so many hours at work together with my boss... I may have had a crush on him, but thank God he's such a man of integrity that we're now good friends instead. I've never trusted anyone the way I can trust him and you with anything I disclose. He's truly one in a million." She felt shame at how she had flaunted herself at him in Scotland and yet he had guided her and become her confidant. "He's the kind of man who makes me believe that romance and true love do exist. You should hear the way he talks about his wife, and the picture of his twin boys on his desk... It's so obvious he's really happy. And I'm glad." She smiled.

"It's so great to hear you talk about romance and love."

"I knew you'd like that. But don't hold your breath." Lauren felt defensive but smiled. Her next thought brought her back to earth. "But I wish I hadn't felt so weak and called the other guy that night after..." Now she would pay for the undeniable consequences for her moment of weakness of texting Vincent to come over.

"I do get it though." Rachel's empathetic smile made her look away from her frank eyes. Rachel had told her that her twenty-six-year-old sister was constantly drawn to the wrong guys, that good men seemed boring and tame to her.

Lauren knew exactly what Abby meant. Did she have more in common with her than she liked to admit? And why did she feel so much older than the three years between them?

Because Abby had never been alone. She'd always had a big sister to look after her. But who had taken care of Rachel while growing up with the mess of a narcissistic mother and mentally feeble father?

She strongly suspected that her friend was hiding much more about their childhood. But Lauren would respect that Rachel had more than enough in her present life than to delve deeper into the past.

What was the use anyway?

The past was dead, wasn't it?

"I still can't believe how easily I've shared everything with you about that night and about my past."

"I'm glad that you're okay sharing it with me."

Of course she hadn't shared Vincent's name, as it was a small community, after all. Thinking about how she had met Rachel, Lauren couldn't imagine her life without her now.

What if they hadn't met in that clinic on that fateful day?

What if... What if she was meant to carry this baby for her friend?

CHAPTER 36

"There's something I've been thinking about, Rachel." She took the plunge into what had entered her mind last night while she tossed and turned in bed. Insomnia had more to do with her deep thoughts than the heartburn after pigging out on the large rack of ribs she had craved at twelve-thirty at night.

Taking in a deep breath and exhaling she said, "I know you wouldn't consider adoption in the past, even as a last resort, but thinking about the way we met at the clinic... it's been like a miracle in itself. And I could not have gone through these past months without seeing you and getting to know you. You're a lifeline." She leaned in closer. "I've been thinking about something and I'll just come out and say it: What if I'm supposed to carry this baby for you and your husband?"

Rachel flinched ever so slightly and then grabbed her hand across the small table. "Lori, it's your baby, you'll love it. Look at how you've become closer to your family, and I promise again you won't ever be alone, I'll be with—"

Lauren shook her head, "No. Please believe me. I'm not going to keep this baby. I know you can't believe any woman wouldn't want this, but I truly am not maternal. Never will be. I don't *want* to be responsible for anyone but myself." She waited for Rachel to really grasp her words. "I'm sorry, I warned you that I'd disappoint you."

"I wish you'd not think like that. How can I be after knowing about your childhood background and getting to know who you are? You're amazing. Of course I understand."

"How do you do it, Rachel? Seeing only the best in everyone? You've gone through plenty with the way your mother ran off with... and the way you had to become Abby's maternal figure when you yourself were only... how old?"

"Grandma Nancy passed away when Abby was nine, I was seventeen, but that's quite different from what you've gone through. You were much younger and you were... alone."

Lauren shook her head and placed her hand on top of Rachel's. Despite her own life-changing dilemma Rachel listened deeply and seemed to truly get how Lauren felt. Yes, true, over the past months of being together, her outlook had swayed towards her own family. She was going to attend her twin brothers' eighteenth birthday party in October.

These days, Lauren even looked forward to seeing them.

But she had never wanted to have children of her own and never would. As she grew bigger, the alien growing inside her made her increasingly sure that she was a loner. That she needed to have her own space and no one dictating her life and decisions.

A man to love her, yes, maybe one day, but no kids. "I'm—I'm being truly open with you. You're so spiritual, why not see this as God's gift to bringing us together and that I'm carrying a baby just for you and your husband?"

Long moments passed and finally Rachel said, "Not only will he never consider adoption," she paused, shook her head and added, "I know him... and although I'm being a coward, afraid to even start the conversation—I have a horrible feeling we won't even get as far as mentioning adoption. He doesn't seem interested in *us*, our *marriage* anymore." Tears liqueied in her beautiful, sad brown eyes. "And maybe it's for the best that I can't..."

She squeezed her friend's forearm as Rachel reached for a tissue in her bag. "Are you sure it's not just lack of communication? You've often told me how loving and understanding he's always been... I can't imagine any man not loving someone as generous and caring as you. And you did say he's been under a lot of pressure at work."

Rachel lowered her head and shook it slowly.

These last few months of having James as her mentor and confidant and Rachel as her best friend put a lot of things into perspective for her. "I've not made this suggestion lightly, believe me. Never mind about romance or love, until you and my boss came into my life I never believed such kind people exist in real life." She swallowed the sudden lump in her throat and pushed ahead. "I'm starting to believe in what you've been saying about destiny and fate. Look at the way we've bonded. I'd never have believed it possible. But you can't keep avoiding the subject indefinitely. Please go and talk to him, and," she hated having to push her, "I'll also take time off to be there when you go in... for surgery before it gets... truly dangerous."

Again Rachel flinched and the pain in her eyes made Lauren wish she knew how to really help her.

Rachel sighed and said in a shaky voice, "I wish I had the guts to just tell him the bloody truth. And how I wish I could adopt your baby!" Her eyes widened at her own admission and Lauren saw her tremble. As if the spoken words could bring on a catastrophe.

She smiled at Rachel's blooming bittersweet smile.

No thunder or lightening.

CHAPTER 37

The art show was incredible. The bold and vibrantly coloured canvasses by Dianna Virtue were uplifting and inspiring. Rachel saw how Abby was affected by her friend's pieces in the high-ceilinged gallery with what looked like over two-hundred guests in the large and airy space.

Despite being distracted by what Lori had told her at the cafe Rachel felt a strange awakening within herself. But if she didn't talk to JT how long could they go on in this limbo?

With a spring in her step, clad in a short, purple dress and high heels, Abby seemed to be enjoying herself, inspired by the artistic ambiance.

As she neared her and Lori, Abby asked, "So are you feeling like some virgin margaritas and pina coladas and some pizza at my place?"

After a moment's hesitation Lori nodded and said, "That sounds great, if you're sure."

Did her sister and Lori know she preferred to stay out longer? She refused to think of going home and facing JT even if Lori's life-changing offer was taking a stronger hold over her thoughts.

She tried to shed the guilt as she drove Lori to Abby's newly renovated place above the café. But the visuals kept getting bigger and brighter and more real.

As Abby showed her friend some new pieces she had been painting in the studio next door, Rachel wondered if it was her imagination or did Abby seem slightly stand-offish towards Lori?

Was Abby jealous of her spending so much time with her friend?

With her own packed schedule in and outside of her busy restaurant, thankfully Abby seemed more content these days. And it was a nice change to be with someone she could lean on and be absolutely transparent with, rather than worry about her sister or upsetting her friends by saying the wrong thing.

Still, she resolved to speak about it with Abby.

∾

Lauren was genuinely impressed with the pieces she had just seen in Abby's new studio next door. It had such a bohemian vibe with the scent of incense and paints and what she guessed was paint thinner in the vibrant colours all over the space. "Dianna's art work is amazing, but I had no idea you're such a great artist yourself." Here in her flat with the fresh paint scent still lingering in the air, Lauren appreciated the warm yet minimal design of the large space. True to her word now that they were back from the avant garde art exhibit Abby was pouring them freshly made virgin pina coladas for Rachel who was driving and the pregnant balloon lady who was glad to be off her swollen feet.

"You're really talented, Abby."

"Thanks. I just wish I'd started years ago, and had more time now. But that's okay. No use regretting lost time."

The somewhat distracted Rachel said, "And it's not as if you're in your seventies." She smiled at her sister who held out her cocktail.

As they lounged on the lovely soft leather sofas and chatted together, Rachel's thoughtful expression made Lauren wonder if she saw more similarities between her sister and her. Or was her earlier offer taking hold of her mind?

"So Rachel explained that you got the café after your uncle left it for the two of you."

"Yes, I was twenty-one and just finished business school, which Rachel had insisted on, and I thought with Kevin, who'd been there since it opened in ninety-nine, I'd learn the ropes. And Rachel had no interest in it."

"It's one of the riskiest businesses to be in, but she took to it like the proverbial duck to water." Rachel's pride shone clear. "She fast-tracked through school and college."

"So you wanted to keep me as busy and on the right tracks." Abby's warm smile made something ache within Lauren as the sisters sat close to each other.

"I wanted you independent as soon as possible."

"If it hadn't been for the fact that we both owned the café together I'd have lost it all to an ex-boyfriend." Abby's lips thinned as she admitted this.

Lauren nodded, "But you're also a smart woman. I appreciate how well you've not just kept up with the trends, but reinvented your brand over and over again. The decor is trendy yet classic. You've made it such a success on your own merits. And you're lucky to have each other."

Abby seemed touched by her words. "Thanks, Lori. I know."

Rachel's heart started to beat erratically; she was so surprised to hear Abby talking about her therapy sessions with Karl, and about their parents. "I kept fighting him about constantly asking me about our childhood when I hardly remember anything. But the last time we spoke about why I think I keep going for the irresponsible, toxic men the therapist explained about how people usually end up in relationships with someone exactly like their father or their mother."

"Like trying to repeat history in your own adulthood?" Rachel asked.

"Well, trying to work through unfinished business with either of the parents. But I didn't see the similarities with our Dad. Do you see them, Raych?"

She considered this carefully and said, "Well, I suppose subconsciously you've been going for someone that you instinctively know won't stay. That he'll prove himself untrustworthy and disappoint you."

"But Dad died. It's not as if he could stop the heart attack." Abby shook her head, "And why have *you* married a man who's nothing like either of our parents?"

"I suppose I got lucky and met someone who made it easy for me to trust in my own dreams." But w*hat if I'd chosen wrongly after all?*

"I remember Brandon. He seemed everything you wanted but you didn't settle for waiting for him to commit. You've always known what you wanted and believed in the happy ever after. Why can't I?"

"But you do, Abs, you've sought out help and ended a bad relationship all by yourself. And these days you seem inspired to..."

"Stay on the right path." Abby's smile flowered as Rachel obviously tried to find diplomatic words. "Well thanks to you, as always."

"Give yourself credit, and Karl also seems really very good at what he does."

Abby turned to the silent Lori who was watching them, "Rachel's been putting together some of the missing parts of the puzzle that is my memory. I'm surprised that I have such a good memory for the present, although there's a lot I'd like to forget." She grinned. "But anything before I was nine, for the life of me I can't remember anything. When's the youngest that you remember?"

"Me?" Lori seemed thrown off for a moment. "I suppose five

or six." Then added, "I remember this one party when I was wearing this lemon yellow dress with white lace across the tummy and how from behind me a boy ran to me on the swing and pulled at my ponytail. When I fell backwards and cried from pain and I think more from embarrassment and my father scooped me up and held me close." The small smile grew as she obviously ran down memory lane. "I'd forgotten all about that. The way he'd made me forget all about the fall within a few minutes. He flew me like a plane until I laughed so much I was afraid I'd puke."

She laughed and she saw Abby's face light up too, "That's so sweet. You close with them?"

"I am now, thanks to your sister."

"Yes, I'm a saint, don't you know?" Rachel grinned, relieved that there seemed to be no strain between her sister and her best friend.

CHAPTER 38

Her office phone rang and even as she answered it Rachel knew who it was.

"Hi, Rachel, missed me? I'm on my way to take you for a fun lunch." He had obviously returned from his latest business trip. Gareth would be pleased. She had declined his persistent lunch invitations over the past weeks, insisting that he deal with Gareth. But obviously Brandon was being Brandon.

"No, thank you. Let me put you through to Gareth, he's expecting your call."

"Not this again, Rachel—"

"Please, Brandon, right now my life is very complicated and I won't lose my job. I need to focus on myself without any extra stress." Before he said that their lunch would help with that, she continued. "Please, Brandon, if you value our past at all, if you really want to be a good friend, prove it. I'm a married woman who loves her husband. Help me, stop making it more difficult and embarrassing for me."

"But you still have feelings for me, I can see—"

"Nostalgia, Brandon. And that's all."

After a long silence Brandon sighed. "I'm sorry. If you ever need to talk, I'm here for you."

"Thank you, I appreciate it."

The relief was short lived when ten minutes later, Gareth stormed towards her and stood frowning over her desk. "What did Brandon Ross mean about not letting you quit? Are you thinking of going to my competitor? Are you planning to open your own agency after all? Or is this about your little fling?" As she shook her head in disbelief, he continued, "I'd appreciate it if you don't start anything you can't finish, especially on my time. He's a client I intend to keep. Have I made myself clear?"

She stood up and stared at Gareth. Her heart beat fast and her face burned as she said, "No... and no. I have no plans to leave and start my own business. And... I'm not having an affair or anything else, even though it's none of your concern. Don't ever accuse me of anything like that again, or I *will* quit. Have I made myself clear to you?"

"You can't talk to your superior like that. I'm your b—"

"I think I've had enough of you and your superiority, Gareth." She opened her desk drawer and leaned in for her bag. "I'm not feeling well. I'm taking the rest of the day off. Right now I don't care if you fire me. In fact, email me to let me know whether you want me to come back at all or not."

Gareth seemed dumbfounded, "What do you mean? Are you really going? But—but I need you here."

A deep gnawing pain grew within her lower abdomen. "I've got to go." Nausea gripped her suddenly and she grabbed the edge of her desk. "But I mean it, Gareth, I won't take any of this abuse from you. I do my job well and I run the office for you, so the least you can do is be civil if you want me to continue on."

"Well, maybe I don't need you now that you've trained Tina to be your own replacement." Gareth looked down his nose at her.

She swallowed. Did she look pale, because suddenly Gareth stared at her and didn't look so sure of himself.

"I don't care about any of it." She walked away and out of the office.

As she entered her car a few minutes later she tried to take in deep breaths but only managed a few shallow ones. Constantly tired over the past weeks, she would get home and rest, maybe sleep a little before making dinner. If JT came home early enough for them to eat it together. She missed him so much but couldn't seem to face him.

Ten minutes into her drive, a sharp pain stabbed harder in her lower abdomen. So deep that she lost her breath and had to brake with all her might and swerve as the car in front of her stopped for a red light. Squealing tires and her gasp reverberated within her brain. She felt a familiar heavy pull from her lower abdomen.

Frantic, she looked around her to see where she could park.

Finally stopped on the side of the road, she gasped and screamed, "No...." as the pain grew inside instead of subsiding. She couldn't do this any longer. But a hysterectomy would end all her hopes completely.

Yet, what were her other options? Why was she risking her life?

At least Lori was risking hers to have a baby. Even if she thought she would put it up for adoption.

At this thought, another agonized cry jerked from within her and she dropped her head on her arms on the steering wheel.

She could never be a mother. Or give JT their own child.

Rachel had to tell JT, but she would lose him now. If they weren't lost to each other already.

~

As Rachel lay on the sofa in the living room, she felt listless. And she couldn't be bothered to breathe, never mind contemplate speaking with JT. Even if by some miracle he came home now, in time to eat the niçoise salad together, Rachel wasn't up to eating much either.

She didn't regret her words to Gareth but imagining herself with no purpose for waking up at least some of the mornings made tears stream down her face. She would go insane.

These days all she kept doing was cry and feel sorry for herself whenever she was alone.

Unsurprised that JT didn't get home until after eight, when she was already in bed, she swallowed the pain killers and tried to focus on the current novel she was reading. But without any luck.

Turning the lights out at nine, she couldn't fall asleep. But she kept her eyes closed when JT finally came to bed.

Eventually, welcome sleep must have drugged her because something warm and sticky between her legs awoke her. The agony in her abdomen and lower part of her body made her cry out.

"It's okay, Rachel, you'll be fine. I'm here." She heard JT's words but was sure it was her wishful thinking.

CHAPTER 39

When Rachel opened her eyes she was in an unfamiliar room. JT held her hand while the beeping, distant female voices and the unwelcome scent of hospital bleach assailed her senses. "No..."

"I'm here, Rachel. You'll be fine."

"They didn't.... JT... Tell me they didn't do a hysterectom—mee." Grasping his hand hard, she stared into his tear-filled eyes.

He shook his head, "No, I knew you'd want Dr. Carter to do it. Even though he's out of town until Thursday. Why didn't you tell me you've continued bleeding?" Tears leached from the inner corners of his eyes. Sad and accusing. "Why have you risked your life like this? You've always told me everything."

"There's nothing you could do, JT. I—I have to tell you something, but please forgive me first." She swallowed through her dry mouth, her tongue so arid.

JT let her hand go and brought a straw to her lips. Oh, how good the icy water felt against them, inside her mouth, down her grazed throat. She drank deeply but started to feel sick. She leaned her head back against the pillows, took some slow breaths and stared at JT. His face had a pasty grey shade similar to his loose tie.

What medications made her feel this strange she couldn't be sure. Despite her heart pounding, the numbness inside her grew. And through the grogginess, the inevitability of what she knew would happen stopped her breathing.

"I can't go on like this." Rachel said after dragging in a ragged breath. Her eyes filled with tears and overflowed as she scrunched them shut.

James stared at his pale wife's face against the white hospital pillows and his heart began to pound hard at Rachel's ominous expression.

"I'm—" The pain in her eyes as she opened them was nearly his undoing.

Rachel started to say, "Three months ago I had the results for the tests I had the last time I went to the specialist."

For some reason, maybe it was her death-row expression, he knew what her next words would be.

"The results confirmed that I—I can never have children. IVF wouldn't work, and I cannot carry a baby to full term even if I..." She gave him the medical terms he'd heard about years ago, that hadn't applied to them before. "The endometriosis has a lot to do with it. And now it's all too late." She closed her eyes as if fearing seeing his reaction. Holding her hand, he inhaled deeply willing her to take her next breath.

James let out a breath that sounded like a hiss. His heart thumped and his armpits tingled. He felt cold and then hot.

"Rachel, I'm so sorry. I can't believe... you've been carrying this on your own all these months... I wasn't there for you." He felt his throat tighten.

The past long agonizing weeks made sense now.

He stared at her. "My poor sweet Rachel. You went to see him on your own... and the tests." He shook his head imagining just how much pain she had suffered. "Have I been... I've been so damned busy at work and helping... other people that I've completely neglected you. You've carried all this by yourself all this time... what kind of a husband am I?"

"I pushed you away, I'm sorry."

"No, I should have been more patient and understanding." That damned stupid dinner party so long ago. Then his workload.

It hurt so much. He couldn't bear to contemplate her agony and suffering over the past months. He thought of the demonic spring cleaning: Her avoiding touching him and staying on in the guest room, and felt even more guilty for not picking up on any of it. And he had exacerbated it with his own work burdens.

He drew her hand to his lips and closed his eyes, his face wet.

"No, please don't cry, JT..."

He'd never cried in front of her.

She let out a gasp, her lips trembling. "I'd imagined seeing only tears of joy when you'd pick up our baby coming out of my womb. And now I can never... I'm sorry, JT. I couldn't bear to...." She inhaled and looked tired.

"I'm the one who's sorry, Rachel. I'm so very sorry."

She sniffed and slowly said, "I know how much it meant to you that we have our own baby and I wouldn't blame you if you no longer want to stay with me."

"What do you mean? Don't you love me anymore?"

"Of course I do."

"I should have been there with you. Not at bloody work. Who gives a..." he nearly swore. "Damn about work if I don't have you? Nothing else matters to me but you." He hesitated for a moment, raking his fingers through his hair and then said, "All these years I've waited for you to agree for us to consider adopting but I knew how important it is to you to have our own baby." He waited for her, scanning her face while holding her hand between his large ones.

"But... but I thought you... especially with your mother... all this time." A small spark of light grew within her pain-filled beautiful brown eyes. He prayed it wasn't his imagination, that something *was* sprouting and slowly blossoming within her. A tiny smile curved her dry lips. Finally her eyes seemed to gain some of that light he hadn't seen for too long.

"I don't care about anyone, I just want us to be together. I didn't know you'd even doubt that. My mother will come round, and if she doesn't I don't give a... damn. So are we going to do this, together, Rachel?"

She nodded, tears blurring her husband's face, but now she could breathe. "Oh my God, JT. All these weeks I've been so afraid to lose you, thinking that you didn't love me."

"I'll always love you, Rachel. I told you that you're my everything... remember that spring night by the fire on those earlier Sundays we used to spend together? I miss them. I've missed you so much." He grinned, feeling his face heat. "You see? How many men talk like that? It's usually the women who are supposed to be the soppy romantics."

Rachel nodded and studied him, her smile growing somewhat.

He kissed her hand and then leaned over her and placed a gentle kiss on her forehead. "Now, let's get you well enough, and we'll discuss other options. Are you sure you can to wait for Dr. Carter? Do you think you'll be okay until Thursday?"

Rachel nodded and knew now that having the unavoidable surgery didn't mean the end of her life and her marriage as she had known it. There was hope, big beautiful hope.

Lori's face came to mind. Had they been fated to meet for a bigger reason than Rachel had imagined after all?

She couldn't wait to text her and tell her that she'd finally come clean with her husband. Lori would be so glad to hear it. Then in a couple of days, she could speak with her and see if she really was adamant about giving away the growing foetus in her womb.

Take people at face value, look at your own husband, whom you'd underestimated so unfairly.

"In a couple of days I want you to meet a friend I met a while back. She's away right now but... if you're sure about adopting there may be a way."

She saw his smile brighten as he said, "Good. I want you happy, Rachel. You deserve—we deserve to be happy, damn it!"

As he held her gently she hugged him back. She'd missed him so much.

She'd been imagining all this rubbish of him not loving her any more when this had been his way of handling pressure. Withdrawing into his work, into his cave, unable to watch her suffer any more.

He loved her. He wanted them to adopt!

Hope bloomed and she started putting her plan in action, how she would call Lori, how she would introduce her to James, and continue supporting her friend and sharing every step of the pregnancy. Wondering if it was a boy or a girl—She didn't care!

Exhaustion was catching up with her. Wallowing in JT's hug, she fell asleep.

CHAPTER 40

Lauren looked pale without make up when she opened the door to James two days later. He didn't know she had freckles. They made her look much younger, with her hair held back in a ponytail.

The stabbing fear in his gut made him stop in his tracks.

"Are you all right?" He asked, coming in.

"Yes, I just got in late last night. What's so urgent that you wanted to discuss it here privately?"

"I wanted to have a talk about my wife Rachel and me."

"I didn't know that was your wife's name. Come, let's have a coffee. Well, I'm having my tea." She sighed.

As she brewed a cup for him he said, "I don't think I've shared this with you before, but my wife and I have been trying to have a child."

Lauren glanced at him with something akin to shock. "You mean in addition to the twin boys?"

For a moment he was confused and then realized she must have assumed the photo of his nephews on his desk were his sons. "They aren't mine, they're my brother's kids."

"So you've been trying to have children..." Lauren looked pale as she asked, "Is your wife's name Rachel Valentino?" She stood ramrod straight, her face even paler than before.

As he nodded she almost whispered, "You're JT."

It started to dawn on him. "Yes... is she the Rachel you met at the clinic and have become close friends with?" He had to sit down on the kitchen chair. As this information registered and took hold of his mind, he breathed through it.

He shook his head, "I suspected but couldn't be sure. This is like a crazy miracle or something. But anyway, on Friday, Rachel ended up in hospital."

"Oh my God, is she all right? Rachel said she had some good news to share with me. I was going to text her later this morning." Lauren sat at the opposite chair across the small square table in the open plan kitchen.

"She was dehydrated and needed a blood transfusion."

"Oh dear God, no. Did she have the... hysterectomy?" Lauren's eyes filled with tears as she held a fist against her mouth.

He shook his head, "I knew she'd prefer to wait for Dr. Carter. He's performing it on Thursday. She says she's feeling much better." He kept it together hoping all this surprise wasn't going to disturb Lauren too much in her condition. "Are you okay?"

"Yes, it's just sinking in. So Rachel told you everything?" She seemed to make the effort to stay calm.

"You mean about the infertility? Yes. And then we discussed our options."

"You've never wanted to adopt..."

"I have never minded it but whenever we've discussed the options, I could see how very important it was for Rachel to have our own children. But she's now considering adoption. That's why I wanted to discuss this...I know it'll be hard for her. But right now all I want is for her to start healing and get stronger."

Lauren's tears continued and she got up, "Excuse me for a moment."

A few minutes passed and she returned with a tissue in her hand and her face looked a little less pink.

"She mentioned about a friend whom she wants me to meet. Now I know it's you. I don't want Rachel disappointed, Lauren. I don't think she can bear any more pain or disappointment."

They stared at each other.

"I've tried to explain to Rachel that I'm not going to keep this baby. But you know her, the romantic idealist, that she's convinced that once I see the baby I'll fall in love with it and change my mind about putting it up for adoption. I promise you that won't happen. Either you and Rachel..." He could see that she was still reeling from the news at discovering the identities of both the people who had become so important in her life.

"If only I'd known about all this I'd have prevented her from going through so much unnecessary suffering," he said.

"I know exactly what you mean. But this is good news, James."

"Yes, it can be if it all works out right." James considered the facts and possibilities and began to let himself feel positive and hopeful.

"First things first, if Rachel's up for a visit, we can meet at our home and discuss things in the next day or so. If she can wait until after the surgery, that may be a better option. She's weak despite her bravado." He swallowed the lump in his throat at how fragile she looked in the hospital bed. "She's determined to come home but I'll see what the doctor says today."

He sighed, "If all this works out I'll be happy knowing that it'll help you as well as us. I've wanted a baby with Rachel for so long...." He glanced at her large belly covered by her fleecy dove-egg-blue bathrobe. "I've let Rachel down so badly I have a lot to make up to her."

He pushed his hair off his forehead with impatient fingers.

"I'm so glad that she's been wrong about... you. Rachel was so afraid that she'd lost her husband. And she even worried he... you were having an affair."

"I can't believe the mess I've created for us both." He shook his head, deliberately shunning the thoughts of what may have happened had he given in to temptation at Wellsley Valley Hotel.

"But this can be the answer to all of our... predicaments. I know you both and you'll work through this easily. You're the only two people who have given me hope about love. Not that I'm interested in any of that," she added.

James got up and looked at his untouched coffee, "I'm sorry, I'd better go and see Rachel."

"Yes, she needs you, and you'll be fine. I know it." This time Lauren's smile was warm and confident.

Why shouldn't it finally happen for them? Maybe Rachel was right all along about God working in mysterious ways.

As Lauren saw him to the door, he inhaled and let himself feel relief and even joy at the prospect of their 'win-win' resolution.

At the door's threshold of her flat, as Lauren opened the door for him James looked back at her and grinned. It unlocked something deep inside him, as if the fear and dread that had been ingrained within him for so long was finally easing.

On impulse he opened his arms and she allowed him to hug her.

"This could make all of our dreams come true. And why not?"

They both laughed softly.

A gasp-like hiccup from somewhere behind him made him tense. Lauren pulled sharply out of his arms, and they both turned towards the lower stairwell and saw Rachel staring up at them.

CHAPTER 41

The truth has finally hit the fan. Everything seemed to fall into place and made perfect sense to Rachel.

Nothing could have hit the mark as well as seeing Lori in her bathrobe and James's shocked and guilty expression.

Unable to move, her subconscious played crazy tracks back to her. Was she still asleep in the hospital bed and having craved their own baby so much, she convinced her unconscious that Lori was carrying James's baby?

No. Somehow Lori's hand over her protruding belly seemed too protective.

Then JT spoke, "Rachel," he started towards her. Still immobile, she realized this was no dream but a reality nightmare that she had refused to entertain even for a moment. All those paranoid niggling doubts and thoughts she had denied made sense. All the jigsaw puzzles of JT's aloofness over the past months, and Lori's "mistake with an unavailable man" came together, and Rachel didn't like the horror picture it made.

But with Lori? She had said she was in medicine, not pharmaceutics. No wonder she hadn't wanted to divulge anything of her present. Did everyone in Oakwood and at Acorn know about the affair, but not the unsuspecting, self-absorbed wife?

To think that until this moment she had allowed herself to hope and believe that Lori had the answer to all her prayers.

Naive, romantic fool.

Now David's bitter words at the gala came to mind. This was the Ms. Mitchell with whom JT had gone away to Scotland over five months ago? How could he have made such sweet poignant love to his wife after having been with another woman in Scotland only hours before?

Had Lori somehow recognized her as JT's wife early on? They must have been laughing all the way to bed. Her blood boiled in her veins, her erratic breathing became shallow. But through it she forced herself to speak. "How could you? Sitting by my hospital bed all magnanimous... letting me think that you're all for adopting a baby... when all along you've been having an affair with... and you," she whispered staring up at Lori. "You horrible, horrible... snake." Her voice was low.

Slowly, she turned away. She had to get a cab and get the hell away from here. From them and what she'd just witnessed.

"Rachel!" Both the traitors said in unison.

"You don't understand. It's not James's baby."

"I've been trying to help Lauren. We never—"

They were welcome to each other no matter the truth or lies. Tears blurring her vision she grasped the cold handrail, numbly putting one foot in front of the other and concentrated on descending out of this building.

She had nearly been manipulated into adopting JT's baby, under the pretence of compromise and love. If they had told her the truth... would it have made a difference? God, how she had wanted it!

Now they didn't need her in the picture. Lori, James and the baby, the perfect family JT and his parents had always expected.

The drumming in her ears was almost deafening as she heard her own chocked hiccups.

As she reached the bottom of the stairs, an urgent hand gripped her upper arm. "Rachel. Wait, damn it."

She turned to Judas, hoping all her hatred showed clearly in her eyes. It must have done, because the yellow-livered lizard seemed lost for words.

"I understand everything now."

"No, you don't."

"Oh, yes, I do! You and Lori, Lauren or whatever her real name is, have had a cozy affair and she got pregnant." It nearly killed her to say the words. "And *she's* carrying *your* baby."

"No. It's nothing like that. Just listen to me."

"No, I was right all along. And now you, your family and everyone will be very happy to have your own biological child."

"I'd never do such a thing, Rachel. You know—"

"Stop. Right now you'll say anything you think I want to hear. But the facts speak for themselves."

"No! They're not facts. That's enough." JT grabbed her arms urgently.

Almost welcoming the pain, suddenly the image of JT and Lori together made Rachel feel nauseated. She felt faint.

She couldn't stand his nearness. She summoned all her strength and pulled out of his grip. "Let me go. Don't you touch me."

Before tears choked her again, she shrugged away his persistent hand as he tried to stop her from leaving.

"I mean it. Don't you dare touch me ever again. It's all over. And you're not the only one who can start afresh. You may not want me but... I have someone waiting for me, too."

Looking at him one more time, she expected to see resignation and sadness...

What she wasn't expecting was the surprise in his widened eyes, his mouth open in disbelief. At his helpless expression, she turned away but he grabbed her again and this time his vicelike arms held her prisoner against the cold walls behind her.

"You'll listen to me first. To the actual truth. And really hear it."

She tried to push at him but felt as impotent as a gnat.

"Lauren works with me and I've never touched her apart from the innocent hug that you just saw. I've never broken my promise to you and never will. Lauren got pregnant after a one night stand with a guy from work, and it's definitely not me! She had no one to talk to about this and she trusted me with her secret, and I helped her, inspired by how I knew *you'd* help her. I had no idea that you knew each other until a few minutes ago. I went to see her so I could discuss the possibility of us adopting her baby, and to gauge if she was really serious about it."

Rachel watched him, and suspicion ebbed away from within her. She did know JT, and she also had a pretty good idea about who Lori was deep inside.

"I can understand how it must have looked just now, and how it made you feel seeing us like that."

Yes, JT and Lori had looked so close and warm and comfortable with each other.

"When she first told me about her predicament, I'd thought it would hurt you if I mentioned her to you. I love you, and only you, and I can't believe that you'd ever think I'd do such a thing. And what hurts even more is that you'd just walk away from our marriage after all the hell we've been going through together. Do you really not know me at all?"

She believed him, but she was so terrified...of what she wasn't sure anymore.

Tears threatened and she lost the battle to keep them at bay.

JT's arms were instantly holding her into him. Minutes passed as she cried then he asked, "What's really going on here, Rachel?"

Snivelling she breathed out, "I don't know. I just need time to be by myself. To think."

"Come and rest in Lauren's place for just a short while."

She shook her head, feeling her warm cheeks grow even warmer. "No, I can't."

"Please Rachel, come up." Lori's voice echoed somewhat in the hallway.

Rachel noticed her friend standing at the top of the stairs as if unsure what to do.

Her phone vibrated and the music told her it was the café. Dislodging herself out of JT's arms she picked her mobile. "Rachel, it's Kevin." He paused before adding, "Have you seen Abby since yesterday? It's just that she's not at home and her phone goes straight to voicemail."

"You've been to her flat and she's not there?"

"There's no answer."

"Okay, I'm on my way." She felt her hands shake as she replaced her phone in her bag's outer pocket and stared at the waiting JT.

"I have to go."

"Let me drive you—"

"No, thanks." She glanced up at Lori and didn't know what to say. "I'm sorry, Lori."

CHAPTER 42

James stood on the stairs for another minute. Then, taking two steps at a time, he reached Lauren's floor and saw her tear-stained face and wide eyes.

"What the hell just happened?" He shook his head, giddy that literally five minutes ago everything was about to work out perfectly for them all.

"It's all right, James, we both know her, she just needs time to process it all. I hope Abby's okay." Then she stared at him and he saw her lower lip tremble. Her eyes moistened, "I pray that I didn't screw it up for you guys. I told you I'm bad news." She retreated into her flat as if blind, feeling her way to her sofa.

"No, I know you're right. She'll come round." He just wished he could breathe properly.

Shutting the door behind him, he following her and paced across the carpeted floor. The headache that had at last disappeared only ten minutes ago came hammering back at his temples and from forehead back to his lower neck.

"I've never seen her like that before."

"She's been under tremendous pressure and it all got too much for her. I don't blame her for misunderstanding…"

He frowned. "What the hell did she mean that there's someone waiting for her?" He pushed his fist into his upper chest trying to stay focused.

"Oh no," Lauren's whisper reached his ears.

Swivelling to face her, he stared at her. "What? Oh no, what?" He leaned towards her, part of him afraid of how pale she looked and the other petrified of what he would learn.

"It's nothing, I'm sure." She shook her head and wouldn't look at him. "I don't know. Just give her some time—"

He sat next to Lauren and said, "Yes you do know, what is it?"

Again she shook her head and seemed to resign herself to say, "Rachel's not working with him anymore... but Brandon, an ex—"

He swore, "No way, not that smooth bastard... I need to get to her... Or have they already...Is that why she wanted to believe all this to make it easy for her to walk away from me? Have they...?" He couldn't finish the thought that made him nauseous and furious.

Standing up he paced again.

"She loves you and she hasn't done anything."

"Yet." His balled fists by his sides; he couldn't see straight.

Lauren rose and stood in front of him. "I know she believed you. I saw her face. She's going through hell, James. Her only dream of having her own baby is gone, especially after this Thursday."

He didn't want to listen, he wanted to find Rachel. Why had he let her go?

"I have to go, but I don't know where..." He got his mobile out. When he got through to Tina, he asked if she had seen Rachel.

"What's happened?"

Now he had worried her. "I'll explain everything later when I know more, but please let me know when you see her or speak with her, so I know she's okay."

CHAPTER 43

Rachel couldn't wait for the cab to get her to Abby's new flat above the café. She prayed that her sister had decided to take a few days away and had just forgotten to let everyone know.

Who are you kidding?

Knocking loudly at Abby's door she heard a slight hum of background music.

Oh, God, what if Abby was in bed with a guy? Better that scenario than worrying about overstepping her boundaries. The prickling discomfort within her grew instead of abating as she let herself in with her spare key.

A strange sense of *deja vu* shook her when noticing a light on in the bathroom down the corridor. Daylight poured in through the large windows.

Dropping her bag and keys as she rushed towards Abby's bedroom door, she threw it open.

"Oh, no, no." She whispered when she saw her sister lying on the bed on her side, fully clothed. The crumpled piece of paper by Abby's still hand forced adrenaline to course through her. Sprinting the few steps to her sister's side she felt her nearest wrist for a pulse. A tiny pulse. She stared at Abby's pasty, immobile features.

Rachel fumbled for her phone in her bag without taking her eyes off Abby's face. "No, Abby, don't you dare leave me... do you hear me?"

~

Over the next few hours by Abby's hospital bed Rachel wished Lori was with her right now. But she had to do this on her own. To sort out her own feelings now that she had finally told JT her long held secret. Everything was out in the open, even if she had jumped to the wrong conclusion about JT and Lori early this morning.

Why had she overreacted like that? What was happening? Hadn't she dreamed of adopting Lori's unwanted baby in the last few months?

She closed her eyes and willed herself to get a grip. She couldn't think straight but right now all that mattered was that her sister needed her.

Distracted by focusing all her attention on the unconscious Abby, Rachel answered her ringing mobile. She heard JT speak but couldn't fathom his words. "I can't talk now. I'm in hospital."

"What?" JT roared into her ear.

"Abby has a fever. She's still unconscious."

"Are you in Whittington? I'll be there as soon as I can." It roused her out of her lethargy.

"No, don't. I'm taking care of this, and I need time, Please respect that. Okay?" She bit her lip, welcoming the pain that was replacing the post-shock apathy. She cut the connection and scanned her sister's peaceful features. JT probably thought Abby had attempted suicide again. Hadn't she herself jumped to that conclusion when she had found her earlier?

The doctor had assured her that Abby would be fine. She held on to that as a lifeline. She would stay with Abby at her flat which had a second bedroom, at least for the next four days until she had the inevitable surgery. But even though Dr. Carter had said it would take five or six weeks to recuperate after the hysterectomy —and therefore too much time to think—right now all she could do right now was take one step at a time and wait until the daze lifted. Then she could think a little more clearly.

She was tired, but more than that she yearned for a nice long soak in a bubble bath, after her own recent overnight stay at the hospital…Did Abby's flat have a tub or only a shower? She couldn't remember.

She needed a hot sweet cup of tea. Beyond that her brain couldn't function.

Later she would text Tina back. JT had called her and now she wanted to know what the hell was going on.

～

*J*ames was losing his mind. After driving himself crazy over the past several hours Rachel had finally answered her phone.

He had imagined her in pain or unconscious somewhere and refused to let the image of her in Brandon's arms. He knew that was his fear and jealousy talking. Rachel was not like that. Yet…

After calling Mac and delegating the long-awaited executive meeting, he left Mac and his team in charge. Lauren had also taken the Monday off, and was at her flat, waiting for him to text or call her as soon as he had ironed everything out with Rachel.

Not knowing where else to go James had driven to Abby's restaurant. The manager told him that Abby wasn't there because she was unwell, the tight ball within his gut went on overdrive. Kevin's curt words saying that Rachel had asked not to let anyone know about it, hadn't helped. If the two sisters were together up on the top flat then he knew Rachel wouldn't talk with him.

He had to bide his time and wait. Knowing how unpredictable his sister-in-law could be he wondered if she tried something stupid again. And if Rachel was with her it could add more stress on her already compromised system.

His relief at hearing Rachel's voice when she finally answered him was short-lived when she told him she was in hospital. He gripped the phone tight trying to stay calm and not add to her stress.

Now early at the Whittington hospital car park he reminded himself to stay positive. She'd sounded tired but as always, was obviously staying strong under pressure.

He strode towards the hospital reception area. On the long drive here, every time he thought of the good looking, sophisticated Brandon he was ready to punch a hole in a wall, anything to stop the images of Rachel and Brandon together.

From the way Rachel had tensed and stared at the damn bastard on their second date in the French restaurant, James should have known there were still embers, ready to be fanned into life.

After having exchanged their vows and promising to stand by each other no matter what life threw at them, had Rachel kept her side of that bargain?

He'd always trusted her implicitly, and maybe that was one of his first mistakes. Taking her and her love for granted in the last few months, he tried to justify that she had become so consumed with wanting a baby that it became a suffocating existence, but he knew that was a poor excuse.

When exactly had Brandon come back on the scene?

James would have loved to know. But first he needed to see Rachel and make sure with his own eyes that she was fine under the circumstances. He also needed to know what the hell had happened to his sister-in-law.

As he rode the lift to the right floor, he remembered how fast he had fallen for Rachel. Within short weeks he had known he would do everything he could to win her love and spend the rest of his life with the fun-loving and ambitious woman. His soul mate in every way.

The duplicity of his outwardly healthy, perfect parents had always been a private joke between them. The knowledge that they both shared the same strong morals of never digressing from the sacred marital bond of trust had strengthened his resolution that no one and nothing would come between them.

But his work had. He had used its pressures to stop trying to work on their love.

No wonder Rachel believed he had lost his way. It hurt to think that she would believe him capable of betraying her and even keeping it secret and staying on in their marriage.

But in her state of such sorrow and with the impending... Oh, God, he couldn't wait to see her and to ensure she was all right. He would be there for her through the surgery no matter what she said.

She could be stubborn, but so was he.

But how could he talk with her and straighten all this out when he feared for her life?

He pinched the bridge of his nose to stop stupid tears from threatening to come. He couldn't lose her, his beautiful soft wife whose only sin had been to try hard to have a baby. To make a family for them. How could he have lost sight of what was most important?

Could he get Rachel back?

More importantly what would it take to earn her trust and love back?

CHAPTER 44

"What are you doing here? I *asked* you not to come." Rachel stood and tried to stop JT from coming into the small two-bed ward. The blinds in the large window shut away the late afternoon sun.

"I thought I'd stay with you until you're ready. Let me keep you company."

She scanned his face as she noted how he studied hers and the resolute line of his lips left her no doubt he was here to stay. That one way or another he was going to get his say and his answers, no matter how long it took.

She turned away from him and with the cold, damp flannel she mopped her still unconscious sister's forehead.

Then putting it down in the ice-cold water she said, "Fine." She sat on the small armchair in the corner from which she had the best sight line to Abby. "Let's talk and then you can leave me alone, just for a few days. I get it, I overreacted, I just need—"

"Time, yes, I know." JT swivelled the chair from beside the bed and sat close to Rachel. Too close for her liking. She folded her arms tightly across her chest and waited.

"How are you feeling?" His astute eyes focused on her even closer.

"I'm tired but fine."

"What happened with Abby?"

"Her temperature was 106 when we got her here, but it's slightly lower now. The doctor's hoping the fever will break soon. But it could take days. From his experience, he says it looks like the symptoms of psychological trauma. I don't know if it's anything to do with the therapist she's been seeing. I've left him a message." She grudgingly looked at her husband and added, "When I got to her flat and saw her on the bed I thought she'd... you know. But thank God I was there. And the note beside her was some kind of list I couldn't quite make out."

"You need to rest."

With her smudged mascara under her eyes, which she hadn't cared about earlier, she probably looked a mess.

As she shook her head, JT said, "Please, Rachel, only three days ago you went through your own trauma and yesterday's... no, let me finish. Yesterday's big misunderstanding most probably left you in shock too. I want you to please get some rest. Even a few minutes. I'll stay here while you go and freshen up and have something to eat or drink."

"No thanks."

"I insist."

"I'm just sitting here and waiting. I want to be here when she wakes up." She glanced away from him. "I don't have the capacity to deal with us, right now. I need you to leave and that will help me more than anything."

When she looked back at him he looked disappointed but then appeared to accept her decision. "In which case I'll just stay with you."

"Oh, please, JT, just go home."

"No." He said simply, like a stubborn boy, folding his arms and settling back.

A guttural sound from Abby got Rachel's full attention. Instantly, she was beside her sister, watching her, praying, waiting with bated breath.

"Rachel." Abby tried to move as if fighting to swim upwards, panting. "I saw it all. It was me. I did it."

"You're okay, Abby. Breathe slowly, you can tell me everything when you're feeling stronger." She gripped her hand and Abby held hers with urgent, trembling fingers. Her head flayed against the pillows, tears ran down her temples, and with a strangled voice Abby whispered, "No. Listen to me... After the hypnosis... that night I dreamt... I saw Mum and this man... she ran away with him. It's because of me that Dad found out... Because of me... I killed our Dad..." Abby seemed spent, her eyes closed tight.

Oh, no. Bloody hell!

Rachel couldn't breathe. Abby's memories were all confused but the gist was true, apart from who was responsible for her father's death. But all this time when she thought Abby was too young to remember any of it, the hypnosis must have jogged it all out to the open.

"I see we're awake." A woman's voice distracted Rachel. She saw a buxom blonde nurse enter the room, calm and in control. "Good." She took Abby's pulse, nodded and smiled. "How about we get the doctor to visit you and your sister can go and have a quick break? Hmm?"

At the fear in Abby's tormented eyes, Rachel said, "No, I'll stay here with her."

Ever since their Mum had run off with the young contractor when Abby was nearly five, and she had just turned twelve, Rachel had been afraid that Abby would remember the past and have questions. But hypnosis must have brought out the memories that her sister was interpreting in her own way, through a small, frightened child's mind. And she was blaming herself?

When six months after Mum had demanded a divorce to stay in France with her new lover, Dad had taken an overdose of sleeping pills and never woken up. Grandma Nancy and other 'adults' had decided to protect Abby with the lie that now Rachel would have to explain in detail. When her sister was stronger.

How much did Abby remember? Had another nightmare brought back that day that changed all their lives?

~

With almost ten days do go before her fifth birthday, Abby had put away all her toys in her princess bedroom so Mummy would be pleased, and now wanted another one of those special crispy cookies. But Mummy was on the phone, giggling. She had never heard her laugh in that playful way, like she was happy, like those grown-ups on the TV shows, before they kissed each other.

She heard her own breathing getting loud as if something in her throat was stopping air from passing through. She stopped in her bare feet around the corner from the kitchen when she heard Mummy talking.

"But darling, I can't help it... I miss you too..." Another giggle. "But he'll be home shortly and I don't want him to get suspicious. Not that he'll care." Silence and then the laughter again. "No, darling, of course I do. You know I do. But I can't till Thursday." Another silence. "Yes, I promise I'll make it up to you." She made the same kissing sounds she used to send Abby on the phone whenever she called Mummy from Daddy's car phone whenever he took her and Rachel out on weekend excursions. "Love you, too." Her voice all breathy and high.

Abby was confused. Surely her mummy couldn't love another man when she was married to Daddy already. She had no one to talk to about this. She knew even Uncle Abe wouldn't like to hear about this. Definitely not Daddy, it would upset him too much and there would be a huge fight, and Mummy would stop loving her. Because even if she said that she did love Rachel, Abby knew that Mummy didn't really like her and now she also knew that Mummy didn't love Daddy.

The sharp pain in her chest brought Abby from her deep sleep and she felt tears on her cheeks as she looked around in yet another hospital room in the here and now.

~

James watched with trepidation as Rachel settled in the chair beside Abby as the sisters held hands.

Slowly he pulled back towards the door. He sighed. He would wait.

Short moments later, a young doctor took over. "Okay, we'll need everyone outside for a short while." Then he motioned to the nurse with instructions for more tests for white blood cell count and other things James didn't understand. Then he turned back to his patient. "And perhaps we can get a few answers, too."

James could see how much effort it took for Rachel to let go of her sister's hand and surrender her care to the medical team.

He was grateful that they were alone as he sat next to her in the small waiting area outside the room. He felt like a selfish heel at how impatient he was to sort things out, or at least talk about earlier today, when Rachel was obviously so anxious and exhausted.

"I know I'm being unfair right now, but Abby's in good hands." He stared into his wife's eyes. She wasn't really listening to him. How could he blame her?

"You need a rest." Now he noticed the dark smudges under her sunken eyes.

She shook her head, "I slept some. This is just mascara." But he knew her. One of the things he loved so much about her was her generosity and caring for others, and how protective she was over Abby.

"I know the difference between when you're tired or if it's

mascara. Come here, lay your head down for just a moment." He gently pulled her head towards his shoulder and couldn't believe how good it felt to have her so near.

"I don't want to sleep; I want to speak to the doctor."

"We will, don't worry." Even as he almost whispered the words, he felt the weight of her head and shoulders relax into him.

Then she slept. He held her and didn't care about how long she needed to rest, and prayed that the hospital sounds of the beeping monitors and staff voices wouldn't wake her too soon.

When the doctor left Abby's side and saw Rachel in James's arms, his voice was quiet as he said, "Ms. Valentino will rest now. I'll update your wife as soon as I've got the test results. But as I'd suspected this may well be connected with psychological trauma. She's very lucky to have gotten help so fast."

When the doctor left, James willed his wife to continue sleeping in his arms.

CHAPTER 45

Banging metal—probably one of those damned bedpans—crashing against the floor awoke Rachel. Almost two hours of sleep in his arms weren't nearly enough. But as she pushed herself out of his arms, he looked deeper into her eyes.

"I told you I didn't—what did the doctor say?"

James conveyed everything the man had explained to him, and saw the instant tension abate slightly.

"I have to stay with her."

"She's being monitored and she'll sleep now. Honestly, Abby's going to be fine."

As she took in a big breath, he saw she was trying to stay strong.

She stood up and stared down at him. "Thanks for coming and," she waved towards his shoulder, "for getting me to sleep. But now please leave me alone."

At least there was some warm hue of colour in her face now.

He rose too and stood before her as his heart hammered inside his chest. "I know you're overwrought with everything but I needed to know that you're all right. And the big assumption about what you saw—"

"It can all wait."

"Can it?"

"You explained it. I get it, I apologize for overreacting."

"We have to get to the actual truth. What's really going on here?"

⁓

The narrowing of JT's appraising glare stopped Rachel from turning away even though she needed to put as much distance between them. She couldn't think about anything other than Abby, surely he could understand that.

"Where does Brandon come into all this? Is he waiting to pick up the pieces?"

She gasped at his feral jealousy patent in his grey eyes. How had he found out? And had he come to the same erroneous conclusion about her and Brandon, as she had about him and Lori?

Even if she had fantasized making love to Brandon in his bed the moments when she had believed JT had betrayed her, she knew she could never have done anything like that. She admitted that all she ever wanted was to have JT's baby. For her to build a family with the only man she truly loved. JT. No one else.

"Have you had an... affair behind my back?"

"No. "We went out for a business lunch... That's all."

"But you never told me anything about it."

"You never told me about Lori." About to turn away, she felt his hand stop her.

"Are you in love with...him?" His voice urgent he suddenly shook his head. "No don't answer that. I don't want to know."

She saw tears in his eyes. He squeezed them shut and raised his face upward.

Rachel, I'm so sorry. I can't help how I feel. I'll try and understand it, but even if you did see... If there's any chance of us working it out I want us to try."

Disbelief made her stare at him.

Was she hearing him right or was she much more exhausted than she admitted even to herself? James loved her so much that even if she had broken her vows to him, he was begging for another chance to resurrect their marriage?

The lump in her throat, which made it impossible to swallow now, seemed to be choking her. He didn't deserve any of this. With any other woman he could have become a father and got everything they had planned and wished for together. The suffering in his eyes was unbearable. But it was all too late.

"No, JT. I'm not in love with him. I love only you..." She took in a breath and let it out at the deep familiar agony pulling inside of her. Continuing studying his beloved face, she reached for him to support herself.

Instantly James was holding her. But his features changed yet again. Relief turned into something akin to panic, concern. Suddenly, feeling lightheaded and drained everything seemed to spin around her.

CHAPTER 46

Rachel felt something ice cold against her lips. They were so dry and she was thirsty but it hurt to swallow.

She opened her eyes, recognized from the sounds and dim lights on the curtains around her that she was still in some hospital.

"Abby!" She wanted to scream but only gagging noises came out of her.

JT stared into her eyes and gently massaged her hand. "It's all going to be fine. Abby's okay and getting better now. And you're now out of danger."

She closed her eyes.

"Can you hear me, Rachel?"

She nodded slowly and let tears stream down her temples. JT was telling her something about Dr. Carter having prioritized her yesterday and that everything worked out well in the end. That she would no longer have any pain or...

No babies. Of course JT wouldn't mention that.

He was saying something about her getting better in a few weeks and then she would start to feel stronger.

Gingerly, she faced away from him and withdrew her hand from his.

"Yes, you need to rest, sleep, darling, I'll be here."

~

A distant cough and a laugh brought Rachel out of a deep satisfying dream where she was lying in a sea of baby's bottles that felt as soft and comfortable as a cushioned bean bag. She heard babies crying in the distance as she came out of the drugged sleep, the warmth within her slowly dissipating.

She opened her eyes and instantly wished she would die.

Squeezing them shut, she didn't want to see or feel anything, because she knew where she was and she wished to go back to her dream. Where there had been some kind of hope. But as she gained more consciousness, she groaned at the deep pain that no medicine could ever reach.

"How are you, darling?" JT whispered from somewhere close. "You thirsty?"

She nodded slightly. Immediately a straw touched her lower lip. She took a tentative sip. Swallowed. Waited for the nauseous grip to ease. Took another small sip and shook her head.

Moments passed. "What time, day is it?" Her words sounded croaky.

"It's Wednesday evening." She tried to remember when she had brought Abby to hospital but couldn't.

"You've been sleeping through two days now. You needed the rest." Was JT trying to sound upbeat?

She looked at him and saw the dark rings under his eyes filled with tension despite the warm smile on his lips. Tears shone in his eyes and she hated herself for having caused him so much grief. She had been stubborn and selfish.

"You've not slept, have you?"

He almost laughed gruffly, "You're amazing, Rachel. Always

thinking of others." He held her hand and seemed to try to gauge if she was willing for him to touch her. She squeezed his fingers slightly and tried to smile.

"Tina was here a while ago. She stayed with you for a couple of hours while I went home to get you some stuff. She ordered me to call her when you're up for company." He looked a little better as they watched each other.

She never wanted to see anyone, but she nodded, "Yes, maybe later. Maybe tomorrow morning... if she's not working."

"She's made you chicken soup the way you like it." JT smiled. "She even forced… I mean gave me some too. Pretty nutritious."

She felt a smile tug on her mouth, "She doesn't put enough salt in it, but I'm glad you had it."

"Now your turn." JT's own smile brightened, "Lemon jelly, apple sauce or chicken soup first?"

∼

Two days later, when she had the male nurse help her up, she felt immense relief that the nurse had taken out her catheter and she could finally use the bathroom on her own.

When she was safely back in the folds of her fresh bed, she lay quietly watching JT sleep in the armchair beside her. He needed it.

If she hadn't dithered for so long and not needed emergency surgery, she would have been sent home by now.

He had refused to leave her side unless Tina was there. Bless her, she had come this morning and stayed with her for hours. "The kids are having a nice time at Andy's parents, and I'm having a break from them." She had said jovially.

Thinking of another best friend whom she missed so much, Rachel must have dozed off because something soft on her forearm made her open her eyes.

She saw Lori standing there with tears streaming down her beautiful face.

A quick glance at JT assured her he was still deeply asleep.

Lori's soft voice was almost a whisper, "I couldn't wait to see you but I didn't want you to be stressed if you still thought..."

"I'm sorry... it all got out of hand." Rachel said.

"I'm the one who's sorry, Rachel. I can only imagine what it looked like. We've both been worried sick but now it's all behind you." More tears made Lori's face redden as she made obvious attempts to stay calm.

"Yes. I'm going home tomorrow." She bit the inner corner of her lower lip when she saw Lori's protruding tummy.

As if telepathic or at least attuned to her emotional state Lori said, "I just wanted to come and say that I'm so sorry to have caused you all this..." Her lip trembled but she continued, "I'm always dragging everyone into my nightmares. I never meant for any of this to happen or to hurt you in any way. I hope you don't cut me out of your life, Rachel. But if you must... I'll accept your decision."

She stood straight and started to turn away. Then stopped and added, "When you feel a little stronger and have had time to heal, let me know what you and JT decide about... considering adopting this baby. Please don't be angry with me because I can't keep it."

Rachel was tired of making everyone around her so unhappy. "It's not just about the baby anymore, Lori." Rachel sighed. She noticed that JT was now awake and watching them from the corner armchair.

"It'll take me time, that's all to get myself in some kind of order and to find myself before I even think about... this." As JT stood and neared her she continued, "I'm still confused about how I feel right now, even though I'd hoped we can adopt..." She swallowed. "Too much time has passed over this year with fear and secrets... First our marriage needs help. But thank you for coming to see me."

Lori nodded, "I'm so grateful for your generous spirit. You've changed my life on so many levels." Abruptly she swivelled on her heels and walked out of the room.

The tense atmosphere between her and JT felt familiar. This proved what she had just admitted to Lori.

"God, Rachel. I can't believe the mess I've made of it all because of my preoccupation at work. How can I make it up to you? Tell me what—"

"Stop blaming yourself. There are two of us in the marriage. All I know is that we can't go on the way things have been."

"I know. You look tired, I'll let you sleep some more." He brought her hand to his lips and stared at her. "We're going to be all right. One way or another." Rachel saw the igniting fire in her husband's eyes, and those passionate lips set in a determined line.

CHAPTER 47

Over the past four weeks since the surgery, Rachel obeyed JT and the nurse he had hired to be with her on those infrequent days when he had to go into London to attend meetings. She found it simpler to just go with the flow.

Often, he worked from his home office and Rachel refused to feel any guilt. He knew what he was doing and her job was apparently solely not to worry about anything but getting better. She slept in most of the mornings and even napped during the afternoons.

Focused on healing and getting stronger, she tried to keep her mind blank.

Despite the physical progress while she forced herself to eat something and walk the obligatory fifteen minutes around the house if the cold weather wouldn't allow her to go out, all she wanted was to be left alone. Which with JT, Tina and now even Abby, she resented how they treated her like an invalid. Watching her like she was a recovering alcoholic.

Oh, God, she was—had become addicted and obsessed.

"So I finally sat her down and explained the situation and my new plan," Abby had been talking to her while Rachel sat in the living room armchair pretending to listen about poor clumsy Nadia. Now Abby wiped her hands on a tea-towel and opened a cupboard to her right. "You're so organized, Raych. Everything has its own place and it's a no-brainer when I think of it. Now I know why I'm so anal about cleanliness, too." She grinned at her across the kitchen counter.

"Thanks, I think." She made the effort to say as Abby brought her a cup of her favorite herbal peach tea even though she hadn't asked or wanted it. She hoped her sigh wasn't loud enough for her sister to hear.

She took a swig of her water bottle and plonked herself back on the sofa nearest to Rachel. "So, what better way than to get Nadia to do what she loves and still feel like she's got promoted instead of put out to pasture?" Abby had arranged for a good hourly rate for Nadia to translate from Polish, (her mother tongue) and Russian, (which she knew fluently) to English at the local immigration centre. "I'm paying for her rehab bills and she loves Lena's massages too. Glad you have some great contacts."

The mention of her acupuncturist massage therapist reminded her of Lori, whom she had referred to her a few long months ago. It hurt too much to think about her.

"I'm so proud of you. That was genius. Kevin must be relieved because his aunt's not one to stay around at home 'resting.' It's borring to stay home." Abby used her hands in an exaggerated imitation of Nadia and her strong Baltic accent. "It's like a prrison to me." Rachel saw the glint in her eyes as Abby said, "There are always options to any problems."

She hoped she wasn't using subtle messages to say something about Rachel's own current mindset. "You're becoming very wise in your twenty-sixth year!" Rachel smiled even though her heart wasn't in it.

"It's not only what you've taught me but with Karl's help, I'm feeling so much better, more confident, you know?"

"I'm glad, Abs."

"Are you tired? Or would you like to watch a movie?" She casually threw the plush blanket over Rachel's knees.

"You're pampering me and you've got your own life."

"You deserve it and I happen to enjoy my new role as your helper instead of always being the one who... you know what I mean." Abby smiled as she leaned over Rachel and kissed her on the forehead.

JT had got into the habit of also doing the same. "I feel like an elderly frail grandma, the way everyone kisses me so carefully."

At Abby's look, she realized she had said it out loud.

"Well, when you're stronger I can whack you about if that's what you're missing."

"Ha, funny." Rachel rolled her eyes. "Seriously, Abs, I'm feeling much better and stronger. You don't have to come and cook and sacrifice your social life by being with me. It's your day off and JT is here. And the nurse comes in if JT's not here. I'm really doing fine." Although she did prefer her company to having JT fuss over her.

"Glad to hear it. If my cooking's that bad then just admit it but don't beat around the bush," Abby challenged her.

"You're obviously fishing for more compliments. If I was up for it, I'd be seriously jealous of how JT makes a fuss about your chicken and your complicated desserts."

"Last night's so-called chicken was spectacular, and for your information it's the original schnitzel cordon bleu recipe as served in Switzerland."

"It's the cheese you put in it. JT will eat anything with melted cheese in it."

"Ooh, how cool! My big sister's jealous of my chicken! You've made my day." Abby sprung up from her favourite spot on the sofa, lay her arm around Rachel's shoulders and placed a big loud kiss on her cheek.

This time, when she smiled, she felt it warm her insides. Her sister was finally growing up. As always, over the past month, any thoughts—positive or negative—made her weepy. But thankfully, her sister didn't seem to notice. But she couldn't be sure, because Tina and JT also seemed to treat her as if she were a deaf and slightly slow elderly person. Within a few weeks, they would all leave her alone.

This made tears stream down her face and she refused to let her thoughts go anywhere near the future.

Take each day as it comes, she reminded herself as she had all those years after her parents screwed up their family forever.

"Oh, did I say something? I was joking, you know."

At this, Rachel almost laughed through her snivelling mess. She blew her nose in a couple of tissues, patted away her tears with a fresh one and took in a deep breath, "You can say or think whatever you want but you'll still never be as good a baker as Grandma Nancy."

"And you." Abby watched her and then said, "Okay, enough of this chit-chatting. I feel like a really funny rom-com. How about you? And James has no say in it." Even before Rachel said anything Abby picked up the remote controls, turned on the Apple TV and asked, "I fancy that classic 'Hitch,' what about you?" Again as Rachel considered it, Abby threw out more names of movies at her.

"You're getting very bossy in your old age." Rachel appreciated her sister's vibrant energy.

"You think this is bossy? Wait till you feel better and I demand all sorts of things from you, *then* you'll see bossy."

Rachel knew this was her way of thanking her again for answering all the questions the hypnosis sessions had brought to the fore in the past couple of weeks. The guilt had been buried deep inside the four-year-old Abby and manifested itself in self-destructive behaviours and not knowing how to break the chains of the habits she could no longer handle.

Putting back many of the missing pieces of the puzzle of

Abby's past nightmares and fears, Rachel was glad that at least she could help someone if not herself.

Abby was becoming a truly self-sufficient contented young woman. Thank goodness she was deriving so much pleasure from her artwork and the restaurant. She was finally starting to see the world with a brighter outlook.

About bloody time, too. She felt tears threaten again, but this time it was from joy, while Abby focused on the next way of distracting her.

CHAPTER 48

SEPTEMBER

Over the weeks that followed her recuperation Rachel began talking with Lori every other day. Although her friend travelled as much if not more these days, now at least Rachel understood why both JT and Lori had such long days and exactly what was going on behind the scenes. JT had confessed that he hadn't wanted to think about work, never mind discuss it with Rachel because he hadn't wanted her to feel burdened or unduly concerned with aspects of what was expected from an EVP at such a large company.

Now he spent more time sharing with her about his work.

"I didn't know you can cook so well, JT." Rachel said to JT as they ate the delicious vegetarian frittata he had prepared all on his own. On this windy fall Saturday evening she wondered if they would ever have that easy romantic closeness they used to have.

"You've spoiled me all these years and now I'm glad to be of service." He smiled and studied her as he always seemed to lately

—cautiously, keeping the fine balance of being caring, warm and helpful without appearing overly concerned.

"Thanks."

He made small talk about work and the new project he was enjoying now that the merger and its drama were behind him. "And so life in the industry goes on, CEOs are replaced by younger, arrogant aggressive executives who only care about the bottom line. Those of us who value our own positions get with the program." She could see he was trying to sound nonchalant and entertaining, but it took all her concentration to keep up with his words. When he mentioned the upcoming TV show they could watch together she started feeling impatient. She couldn't tell why.

She swallowed the small mouthful of the freshly baked bread he had bought from the freezer section at Waitrose and baked perfectly, and put her knife and fork down.

Instantly, he looked at her as if on full alert.

"It's been over seven weeks and I feel well enough to drive now."

"Okay, if you're sure, that's great." He watched her expectantly. But what was she thinking? She wasn't sure what she wanted, what she needed from him or life itself.

As if aware of this while she tried to form a sentence, he said, "I don't mind continuing to stay in the guest room until you're ready to talk, really talk. You're comfortable enough aren't you? Is there anything else I can do to help you?"

She shook her head and he looked disappointed. She added, "You've been wonderful."

After a pause he said, "If you're sure you're strong enough," he couldn't seem to find the right words. "Then I'd like you to consider Dr. Carter's recommendation. A marriage counsellor. Would you let her come here to speak with us? Or we can go to her office. I was waiting to ask you about it but I wasn't sure if you were... ready to talk yet."

He picked up both their plates even though she hadn't quite finished her salad and frittata—or had she?—and strode into the kitchen.

Minutes later, he returned and sat down, his jaw tense although he seemed to have recovered his composure somewhat.

"All right. Here or at her office will be fine. Up to you."

The bittersweet relief within James was enormous. "Thank you." He said like he was a stranger communicating carefully with someone who just wanted to be gone. Gone from his life or from life itself? He tried to smile to keep things light, but it wouldn't come.

Helpless and impotent, he wished he could breathe hope or some kind of emotion into his apathetic wife.

He knew he was being unfair and impatient, but it hurt to see her this numb, this disinterested in life. What would it take for her to accept that he meant every word he said, that even if they never had children together as long as she was with him that was all he wanted. He needed her. It cut deep within him to see how broken she was, but damn it, they had each other, they *loved* each other.

Wasn't that enough for her anymore?

~

Dr. Carol Eisen wasn't what Rachel had expected, but neither had she really thought about this session or how she felt about the shape of the future and their marriage. But JT deserved to have a chance to really feel heard. As mid September offered up cooler evenings, she kept counting the weeks of Lori's pregnancy. Was the time passing as slowly for her friend as it was for her, despite her many hours of 'rest'.

Lori was in touch often and she missed seeing her but she couldn't bring herself to invite her over. She wasn't sure she was strong enough to see her friend and her growing belly. She would be even bigger by now, Rachel was sure, going into her sixth month.

Having put on some makeup with unsteady hands this morning, she focused on just surviving the day. She wanted to sleep more, to just stay alone. Like each long day over the past weeks since she had finally woken up without her womb or tubes... or hope for anything.

She tried to concentrate on the here and now as after the preliminary introductions Dr. Eisen invited them to explain what issues had brought them to see her.

Rachel didn't know where to start or what to say. She looked to JT whose shoulders dropped slightly and even as he tried to hide his disappointment, she was relieved he started speaking.

He explained that their marriage had been a strong and close one until last spring, and gave the doctor the condensed but accurate version of how his work responsibilities had become overwhelming and that he had become impatient with Rachel's need to get pregnant. He shared about how hard it had been for her with his low sperm count and the many invasive tests to help with resolving their infertility issues.

"Rachel braved them all. She wouldn't tell my family the extent of the unexplained infertility we were trying to overcome. And to add to it my mother is not the most sensitive or emotionally intelligent person, which put extra pressure on us both, especially Rachel. I wasn't there for her, then I stopped trying in our marriage."

When he explained his work and mentoring relationship with Lori, whom he of course called Lauren, Rachel understood far more about how hard he had tried to figure out ways to help the young woman while wishing his generous-spirited wife could help.

"But while she appreciated my help and listening ear about her choices with this unplanned pregnancy, I was more concerned about protecting Rachel. I didn't want anything to hurt her, including being faced by the unfairness of life dealing with this situation."

He talked eloquently about the morning when they all discovered each other's identities and Rachel's misunderstanding. There was no blame or resentment in his voice or his face as he described what he had most feared that day. "All I cared about was her safety and that she wouldn't end up in hospital somewhere, alone without me by her side." He seemed to need a moment to stave off the memories that caused a break in his voice.

CHAPTER 49

"This brings us to the present." He soldiered on and something within Rachel pinged and tingled. But then it was gone. "Of course I understand that it's been a hard time. I can only imagine how it feels... and I'm really concerned about her withdrawn state since the surgery. And years ago Dr. Carter had warned us of the various pitfalls of the journey to trying to... become a family. The pressures that could cause major issues in a marriage no matter how strong. I fear that Rachel's getting too depressed."

She recognized the intense worry—had he been trying to cover it all up these weeks?—was now clear on his face. Or had she just not seen it?

She stared into his vulnerable eyes. "I'm not depressed, just tired and sluggish." Even though both the doctor and JT waited for her to say more, she was out of words.

When Dr. Eisen asked him a question that Rachel missed, she was taken aback again by JT's response. He explained about how he saw their current stalemate situation taking all responsibility for everything that she knew was in fact *her* fault.

"So we're here because while I'm giving it as much time as

Rachel needs to heal, physically and emotionally, I'll do anything and everything to help her recovery." JT took her hand and slowly added, "I know you need time, but... It tears me apart that you still may think that without a baby we don't have a marriage. We have each other, Rachel. I love you and you're my everything. I'm so sorry for having let you down when you needed me most." At his moistening eyes, her ever-ready tears broke.

She looked down at their intertwined hands and couldn't speak. A part of her knew she couldn't hide forever behind the temporary reprieve of her now longer hair that framed her face. But she still had nothing to say.

After a few moments, Dr. Eisen spoke. "Rachel, you seem surprised at what you've heard James say just now. What's most surprising for you?"

Slowly Rachel raised her head and looked at the doctor. "That he thinks it's all on him, when I know it's fully my fault." She forced herself to add, "I stopped trusting in us, I kept the results of my infertility a secret for months..." broke down, unable to go on.

JT held her and rocked her as she sobbed into his jacket.

She stayed immobile, her eyes closed. A glass of water was offered to her. When she finally saw it, she held it carefully and sipped slowly. Minutes passed.

Annoyed at her weakness and show of such uncontrolled emotions, Rachel tried to continue. This was not depression; she had grown up with a father who had truly been depressed. And even Abby up to a few months ago.

She was made of stronger stuff.

Turning to JT, she said as calmly as she could, "I'm not... I may be feeling sorry for myself right now, but I think.... I'm healing, and I get that it'll take more time. But I'll try harder at making our marriage work."

She saw relief in his eyes.

"All I want is for you to be truly happy," he said.

"What do you think would make your happy, Rachel?" Dr. Eisen asked.

"I don't know." She answered honestly. Only weeks ago the hope of perhaps adopting Lori's baby had kept her going. But... "I'm afraid it's unfair on you if you could still," Rachel looked at JT and bit her lower lip before she got sucked down into the deep well of darkness she was adamantly fighting. "Are you sure you'd not rather have children with someone else?"

"After all these years don't you believe me when I say that I don't care for anything or anyone but you, Rachel? I don't want to ever have children if I can't have them with you. I only thought that it would have helped both Lauren as well as us if she was willing to let us adopt her child." He studied her face and added, "You'd seemed to be happy when we'd discussed adopting."

She delved deep inside herself and wondered what had shifted within her and why? From the doctor's frank expression and JT's expectant look she knew she had to say something. Taking in a deep breath and exhaling she said, "I'm so scared. I don't want to hope again and then lose the chance...What if Lori decides to keep the baby when she has it?"

"There are no guarantees but you've got to know her and I believe that she truly doesn't want to keep it." Something opened up within her heart and more tears flowed down her face. But this time she could breathe a little easier. A sliver of anticipation warmed and bloomed inside her. JT knew Lori too.

After long moments of silence, Dr. Eisen sat forward slightly in her high-backed leather chair and said, "You're both suffering immeasurably. It's obvious that you care about each other very much. Take some time to consider the things discussed here and continue widening the communication path to each other. Would you like to see me in a few days? Because I think you've both had enough for today."

JT looked disappointed but then nodded.

CHAPTER 50

Under their protective umbrella as JT manoeuvred Rachel into the car he asked, "Are you tired, do you need to rest, or would you mind stopping off somewhere first?"

She wasn't sure how she felt but nodded, "Okay, where?"

"Let's see if you can guess." She found herself liking the hopeful smile on his face. God, how had she forgotten over the past months how adorable her husband was? Or had she been too self-absorbed as usual?

As they drove away leaving central London behind, the rain became worse. It was only two o'clock in the afternoon but everything looked grey and miserable.

When something awoke her, the car clock told her that she had slept for thirty-five minutes. Looking around her, she guessed where they were headed as JT turned his car on to the cobbled country road. Up ahead she saw the church where they had been married over eight years ago.

Rachel felt goose bumps tingle through her whole body, her breath constricting in her throat once more.

"Is this okay with you? I thought..."

"This is wonderful, JT."

Tears sprang in her eyes. Under the large umbrella with his protective arm around her, JT led her inside the church. When he relinquished the now sopping wet umbrella by the huge inner doors, they entered deeper into the dark cold interior. The musty smells reminded her of old libraries and books and moss-covered ancient stones. And her grandmother's love of churches.

It was far too long since she'd entered a church. She felt like a traitor for not believing and having lost faith in everything and everyone around her.

JT took her hand as they walked up the aisle to the altar. She stared up at the jewel coloured leaded glass windows, which sparkled despite the ominous weather outside. Their echoing steps made her conscious of their aloneness.

As they reached the pulpit with the dark red velvet carpet where couples joined in front of the priest and God, JT turned to her with a tender smile.

Some dim, warm lights came on above them, shedding romantic gothic shadows on the ageless stones and wooden carvings. The multi-coloured dome-shaped windows were luminescent, adding a bittersweet atmosphere to these moments.

Clasping both her hands within his, JT stared down at her, sombre and intense as he had on the day they had exchanged their vows.

"I love you and here in God's house, I swear I always will. And I'll spend the rest of our lives proving just how much if you hold on to the faith in me, in us. Over the past months I can see how it's been shaken, but you're the most positive and determined person I've ever known. I've let you down and I'm so sorry. You make this sometimes ugly world beautiful. I meant what I said back there. You're my everything." Even in the gloominess Rachel saw the passion and determination in his eyes, and heard it in his every soul-replenishing word.

He waited as if gauging her feelings. Then when he looked like he wanted to say more she reached out and gently touched her index finger against his lips. Those lips, which she realized she had missed for too long.

Were her eyes betraying her reawakening emotions? Because once more, his sigh held obvious release. He scanned her eyes as if divining for more, waiting for her to come back to him.

"Thank you. I feel it. And I love you, too. I realized it frightens me at how much I do care about you, about us. But it'll take a long time with a lot of effort on both our parts to make this work. You realize that, right?"

"Yes, and I'm fully committed to you forever, for as long as it takes. Believe me, nothing will ever get in our way again. I want you happy and that's my whole purpose in life."

When she was about to argue the point he shook his head and said, "Please, Rachel, trust in us and we'll be fine, even if we're a work in progress. I promise you."

Slowly she nodded, "I trust you."

"Do you think seeing Dr. Eisen the day after tomorrow is too soon?"

She shook her head and a smile formed on her lips, lightening something dormant within her. "I think that will work."

As he stared at her mouth she felt heat rise from her chest up her throat and to her cheeks. Tentatively JT leaned in and brought his lips closer to hers but stopped as if waiting for her agreement.

She pulled closed the space between them weaved her arms around his waist and kissed him softly.

The sound of a long held groan and what sounded like a chuckle from within JT's chest reverberated against hers. He held her gently as if she was a delicate doll, and felt somewhat frustrated. Then immediately remembered that he was giving her the physical and emotional space she had asked for.

She held him tightly and let herself feel, receive and just be. He seemed to be right there with her, completely attuned to her needs.

Long silent moments passed before she pulled away, looked at him without letting him go, and said, "And I'd like to have Lori over, too. I've missed her. It would be nice to see her. I just realized that she's never been at our place before. I'd always ended up in her flat or meeting up somewhere else..." Rachel said in a casual way.

"Of course, I'm sure she'd be delighted to visit. If you're sure."

He nodded, still holding her, curiosity and such sweet hope on his face made her smile grow, and she derived even more faith just by being in his arms.

"Now I have a favour to ask of you." She whispered very close to his ear, "Can we get out of this cold place and get a hot chocolate?"

As his laughter echoed around them, she placed her head on his chest, as close as she could to his heart. And for the first time in what felt like years, she breathed in deeply enough to accept and take into herself the rejuvenating power of their togetherness.

With Dr. Eisen's help, she would learn to once again be happy with JT without expecting anything more from herself. And she would trust Lori's words.

CHAPTER 51

OCTOBER

When Lori came over for coffee the very next day it was like they had never been apart. Rachel was taken aback at the weight Lori had gained since they'd seen each other outside her flat in September. Now at over seven months pregnant she looked heavy and uncomfortable in her skin.

"How are the headaches, Lori?"

Her friend waved her question away, "Some days are better than others, but I'm not concerned, and you shouldn't be either. I just have to stay off my feet, that's what makes it more frustrating." Her ankles were swollen and her face seemed puffier. "And the amount of pee breaks I have to take, you wouldn't believe." She smiled, as if trying to keep it light and unimportant. Rachel let the subject go divining from the expressive hazel-green eyes that she preferred to talk about anything but the pregnancy.

"How's it going with Abby and the therapist?"

"She's getting there. It's still not easy, but she's still here with me ostensibly in case she has more nightmares, but you and I both know she's just here spying on me."

Lori laughed softly, "Yes, Tina, James and Abby—oh, and I, of course—all have a hidden agendas to keep you here like a prisoner."

"Well, thanks for not saying like an invalid or nutcase." Rachel smiled and felt something relax deep within her.

Take each day as it comes. You have a lovely life and it could have been worse. Gratitude will go a long way to help you heal.

"Only because I didn't want you to call me out on anything about my hefty weight gain. You know when people say 'the elephant in the room'? That's me right now. Because I know I look and feel like a huge mammoth!"

～

On the following therapy session in Karl Muller's office, Rachel felt a definite sense of progress from the way Abby started opening up more about the past. Unsure what was real and what was fear or imagination, Abby would describe to Karl what she remembered, and often looked to Rachel to fill in the missing pieces and gaps from their childhood.

Over the last few sessions what had unfolded through the portal of her sister's memories shone a bright light for Rachel to understand why certain things triggered problems for one sister but not the other. Same memories in the same place with the same parents, but different vantage and view perspectives.

"What do you remember about the time you were around five?"

Abby started recounting thoughts, unravelling further layers like she had over the past few weeks.

～

A week after overhearing Mummy's confusing telephone interaction, making kissing sounds to someone called Armand, the nearly five-year-old Abby opened the front door to enter her home and in the far end of the corridor in the kitchen she saw a tall man with his chest uncovered pushing himself away from Mummy. As she stared at her mother's pink cheeked face the big man fumbled as he fastened his shirt buttons. "Ah, thank you, Mrs Valentino, for drying my shirt when the water spilled all over it. I suppose I'll leave you now." He rushed past her and Abby would forever remember that sharp lemony smell mixed with how trees smelled in the forest.

"Where's Rachel?" Mummy stared at the door as if afraid of something.

"She told me to tell you... She's with Jessica next door for a while."

As Mummy touched the stranger's upper arm Abby just knew that this was the man from the phone, Armand. She didn't like him or the way he looked at her Mum.

"You'd better go before she..." Mummy stopped talking.

Within a few days Abby had withdrawn from the rest of the family. Dad began worrying about her waning appetite and listless behaviour. Often she stayed home sick, needing to make sure that the man didn't come back. Her best friend Sarah's Mum and Dad had divorced a few months ago and now there was a new boyfriend who smoked and scratched his big belly while watching TV. She didn't like going there anymore.

Abby's sudden regression, wetting the bed, clinging to Rachel and Dad Mum lost her temper when Abby refused to dance. At first Mum tried to be patient, not pushing her to practice or go to classes. However, as the 'brooding' days stretched into weeks and she missed too many classes due to feeling sick or too tired, Mum's frustration grew.

Now her lovely smiling mother was threatening, "You'd better stop whatever it is you're doing, young missy. You're going to shape up and do what you were born to do, you hear me?" When Abby just stared back at her and nodded Mum hissed, "I don't know what's got into you, but I'm not standing for any more of your nonsense. I've worked too hard to get you into this program, you ungrateful child, and you'll jolly well just get back on stage. And you'll perform perfectly this time!"

Abby no longer thought her mother beautiful. Before she could hold it back she leaned forward and vomited all over Mum's high heeled shoes. She burst out crying when her mother grabbed her by the arm and pulled her towards the toilets. "You did that deliberately, you spoilt brat. I'd thought at least you'd turn out differently instead of dragging everyone down.

Abby didn't understand why other mothers seemed nice but not hers. Her mum was mean to Daddy, and ignored Rachel almost all the time. As long as Rachel did as she was told, Mum left her alone, lavishing all her attention and compliments on Abby. But not after she was sick over her Mum's shoes.

Abby loved and admired her older sister. She seemed so strong and not afraid of their Mum, always knowing what to do and when to placate Mum so she would not get angry with Abby or Dad.

Abby didn't wonder until later why Rachel didn't mind Abby being the favorite. Daddy's love appeared to be enough. Daddy, who worked long hard hours, had plenty of love and time for both of the girls, but not for Mum. Mum didn't work but these days she no longer had time for Rachel or Abby.

Her first panic attack happened on stage at the prestigious ballet school at the end of school year. She was an angel bringing some sad news to the little prince, trying to save him by showing him to safety. She was supposed to fly a few feet above the ornately prepared stage. She was so frightened of being sick, she couldn't catch her breath.

Her mother's words kept whirling through her brain.

Before the show had started Mum had told her that she looked so beautiful in her candy pink outfit, and the gossamer wings were perfect for her little angel. Adding, "You know how important this evening is. Everyone is counting on you to do a wonderful job, so you'll get noticed. You may even get the lead role next time. Mummy loves her little angel," she had kissed her cheek, careful not to smudge her own lipstick.

Abby remembered the waft of that delicious floral perfume, as Mum walked away. Would she come back, or was she going to go away with that other man? Shaking, she stared at the rising curtain and the thousands of faces looking back at her and the other fairies and angels.

What if she couldn't remember her lines, would Mum get mad at her like she got mad at Daddy? Would she leave them all? As silence replaced the noisy applause in the now dim theatre, she looked down at her shoes. Suddenly she couldn't breathe so well. She wondered what would make her Mum angrier; her forgetting her lines, or her being sick all over her pink dress?

~

Karl was so admirable and patient at bringing it out in a controlled and safe way that Rachel was glad Abby had his support. He studied Abby's face with his deep compassionate grey eyes and said in his deep low voice and heavy German accent, "It'll take time, maybe months or even years, but you'll no longer feel enslaved to the past. I know how impatient you can be, and I'm keeping you accountable, but stay real, and remember that you cannot rush this process." Bringing his astute gaze to Rachel he added, "I'm grateful for all your help, Rachel. This process would have taken much longer otherwise. So continue reminding your sister to stay patient and, of course, fill in the rest of the missing pieces. In the meantime go on with the here and now. We're all a work in progress and never stop learning."

CHAPTER 52

NOVEMBER

The phone rang on Rachel's nightstand at 5a.m. and Rachel swore that if this was a wrong number or yet another telemarketer, she would have the landline disconnected.

"Dr. Carter here, how are you doing Rachel?"

"I'm... fine, thank you. Doing well." She was thrown off by the unexpected caller.

Over the past few weeks since after moving back into their marital bed even though JT and Rachel hadn't made love yet, the skin to skin closeness and the togetherness was helping her heal in tandem with their sessions with Dr. Eisen. This past Sunday their romantic and easy evening in each other's arms in front of the fire made her hopeful of one day soon making love with JT for purely feeling connected and feeling as one. She was starting to feel healthier and stronger. No more periods. No more pain again. And for the rest, time would unfold what was meant to happen about Lori's baby.

"I'm sorry to disturb so early in the morning but this can't wait. Ms. Lori Oliver has you on her emergency call list. She's also asked if you can come. I've been briefed on the connection between you two and we need your help."

Rachel was wide awake. Fear snaked around her whole body. "Is Lori all right? Is it the heart or the high blood pressure?"

The hesitation was very short before Dr. Carter said, "Actually, her heart's not too bad, but it's preeclampsia. And there are complications from the high blood pressure, which are now an issue. She says she needs to see you before consenting to have surgery."

"I'll come—We'll come right away." She confirmed they were in the Royal Free Hospital and where to go.

Beside her JT sat up in bed waiting for her to update him.

"Lori is in emergency and has asked to see me. May we...?" She couldn't trust herself to concentrate on driving or seeing Lori and the specialist on her own.

"Of course. Let's go."

Before the sun had even risen, JT drove through the eerily quiet roads with a sense of urgent purpose.

"She's not due for another six weeks, JT. Why hasn't she told us what was going on?" Fear and trepidation crushed her heart. "Had she confided in you so I wouldn't worry? Has the travelling been too much for her?"

"She hasn't said anything to me. We'll see how we can help, so stay strong, okay?"

Finally standing by Lori's bedside, she couldn't hold back her tears. The slumbering Lori looked way too pale.

What had she been going through over the past few months in silence on her own, while Rachel had wallowed in self-pity? Yes, she had lost any chance of having babies but she was alive and getting stronger with each day. This woman had been adamant in having this baby despite the risks. Yet another unwelcome legacy from her mother's side of the family.

She heard slight footsteps and saw Dr. Carter by the door. He motioned for them to join him outside the room.

He quickly updated them that for the past five weeks Lori had been under their care and because of the preeclampsia the situation was too dangerous for her and the baby, who was in distress. "But she refused to have emergency surgery until she could see you. Time is of the essence and we have to perform a caesarean immediately. The nurse will stand by and I'll be back in a few minutes once you've spoken with Lori."

Rachel nodded and worked up her courage to help her friend in any way she could.

When Lori opened her eyes at Rachel's touch on her arm the relief she saw in those pain-filled hazel-green eyes made her throat tight. Lori's pasty colored skin seemed even more pale against her mussed red hair crowning her head on the pillows.

"How are you doing, Lori, or is that the stupidest question ever?"

Lori smiled weakly and tried to hold her hand. "I'm glad you're here. I'm so sorry if you're still not up to it, I was hoping you'd have more time to think... I can't even do this right... I'd hoped that it would stay in me till it was safe to... But I pray it's healthy... but it seems this baby can't wait to see this world."

"Lori, they have to do a C-section right now, do you understand? Your life is in danger. What is it that you need? I'm here, we're here."

Glancing at JT and then back at her, Lori said, "I still believe... it was all meant to happen this way... and that this baby is meant to be yours and James's."

Afraid to believe, but fearing for her friend's life much more, she held Lori's hand and said, "Okay, but first will you let them operate?"

"Promise me that no matter what happens to me, you'll adopt the baby. I'll make sure it comes out... healthy." Lori slowly glanced towards the machine, which threw out small even beats.

The baby's heart monitor, Rachel gathered, but continued studying Lori's pale face.

"Don't talk like that, please, Lori. None of the drama, all right? We're here now and you'll be fine, do you hear me? I want you to stay strong and you'll pull through this. And you'll never be alone again."

Lori nodded and her tears and wobbling chin reassured Rachel enough for now. She breathed a little lighter as she turned to get the nurse and saw one come through the door. As the nurse quickly moved tubes and machines around and prepared to wheel the bed out, Lori wouldn't let Rachel's hand go.

Rachel braved a big smile and said, "Stay with me, okay? We've still got way too many things to gossip about, once you're done here. So go and prove what strong stuff you're made of, just like Aunt Agnes always told you. And come back here with a healthy baby. Promise me now."

"Okay... but I need you... I want you and James in there with me to be the first to see the baby, to hold it."

She had expected that to be the worst nightmare of her life, to see the baby born and then lose it, but instead the desperate request somehow felt absolutely right and perfect. Rachel smiled and let her tears gush out. Other than getting Lori out of danger immediately, there was nothing she wanted more than to see the baby.

She forced herself to answer through the painful airways, "Yes, Lori, this feels right, and it'll be our honour."

Lori seemed to relax and Rachel saw more tears trickle down her cheeks and temples. She heard her sigh as Lori's hold on Rachel's hand eased somewhat.

Then it went limp.

CHAPTER 53

Once Rachel and JT were prepared for the operating room and with their medical masks on, they each stood by Lori's side with the blue drape divider above Lori's stomach closing away their view from seeing the procedure.

Dr. Carter motioned to the anesthesiologist and Rachel felt nauseous and yet positive. She had to stay positive. Lori would be absolutely fine. They had too many things still left to talk about, to do together, to share with each other.

And she would open her heart to Lori and adopting the baby if that was her wish.

Because if this was God's gift to her and JT, then she would stop fighting herself and welcome it with open arms. But right now, her friend's life was on the line.

Having had the same procedure for her hysterectomy just over two and half months ago, she found it difficult to be on this side of the operating table. She stared at her unconscious friend, thanked God for small mercies that she was under general anaesthesia and continued praying hard.

As every second seemed to move extra slowly, she resolved to be Lori's strength now and for as long as she was needed. She glanced up at JT and reminded herself that she was no longer alone. They would do this together. His grey eyes studying her over his medical mask told her to stay strong too. That he loved her and that it would all work out.

From the lower part of Lori over the draping partition, a flurry of activity caught their attention. Dr. Carter held a tiny, blood-covered baby as the nurses made quick work of cleaning off the blood and white sticky substance over it.

It was so very small and it made no sound. Was it okay? Wasn't it supposed to cry?

With quick-measured actions, the two nurses finished cleaning and wrapping the baby as Dr. Carter said, "It's a healthy boy. He's jaundiced and his lungs aren't as developed as they need to be but he should be fine soon with a short stint in the NICU, I mean Neonatal Intensive Care Unit." The baby had a thick tuft of dark orange and blonde hair on its tiny head.

Glancing quickly at Lori's still form, Rachel asked, "Lori. How is she?" She was trembling and was glad to feel JT's sturdy warmth behind her as he grasped her upper arms.

"We'll know more once we're all done here." He offered the small bundle to her with an inviting smile. "Lori wanted you to hold the baby."

As Rachel stopped breathing and slowly opened her arms, the most incredible feeling washed over her. She felt the lightness of the baby and as she stared down at the crinkled little face with its tiny features, puffy eyes and large ears, she dared breathe out.

"Are you sure I won't hurt him?" She blinked fast so the tears wouldn't stop one single second of feasting on the beautiful little soul in her arms. She brought it against her bosom like she had dreamed for too many years.

"A few minutes will be fine. The bonding is more important than anything else right now." Dr. Carter explained with a smile that reassured her.

She was totally in love with the little being with the pink lips that seemed to divine towards one of its minuscule fists and started sucking on it.

Rachel leaned into her husband who was supporting her weight and she heard a throaty sound that vibrated from deep in his chest.

She gave him a quick sideways glance and turned slightly and ever so slowly so he could see and touch the baby too. JT seemed as shaken as she felt and knew from his face full of emotions that he, too, was enthralled with the magic of this miracle.

Their own miracle baby.

~

What seemed like hours later, Rachel and JT sat in the waiting room and she prayed and waited to hear the doctor's prognosis of Lori's recovery. Although the euphoria of having touched and held the baby was keeping the warmth and the hope alive within her, when she saw Dr. Carter striding towards them an hour and a half later, the serious expression on his tired face made her heart hammer.

"Lori has had a seizure and we had to give her another blood transfusion. She's now in a coma."

"No." Rachel gasped. "Can you... what can you do for her?"

"We'll monitor her progress and we should know better in the next twenty-four hours."

"How can we help? Can I see her or is it better... what can I do?" She knew she was starting to panic but she couldn't just sit and do nothing. She would go crazy. And Lori needed her.

"It may help if you stay with her and talk to her." Dr. Carter reached for her hand and patted it. "We're doing all we can and you've both been of great help."

She appreciated hearing it but was impatient to get to Lori's side. As if aware of this, the doctor told her the nurse would take her to Lori in the ICU.

The intrusive sight of the tubes and the beeping surrounding them added to her overwrought system but Rachel focused solely on Lori. JT stayed with her silently.

Slowly she whispered, "Lori, I'll touch your hand now, okay? Here it is, nice and gentle just like you'd held my hand on that day at the clinic." She softly stroked Lori's cool hand and a shudder went through her whole body. She wouldn't let her friend leave her. She continued talking in calm and deliberate tones, which she hoped would reach those deep parts of Lori's psyche.

"You've done an amazing job, Lori. The baby's absolutely perfect." She let tears come and didn't stop even when they threatened to break her voice. Her feelings of love, gratitude and fear for her friend's life were all part of who she was. Lori knew this and would accept it all, she hoped. "You were right when you said that we were meant to meet each other that day. You know me better than almost any other woman in this world."

She didn't realize that JT had left and returned until in her peripheral vision, she saw a mug of a steaming brew that smelled of delicious hot chocolate.

She smiled into his eyes, "Thank you, my lovely hero." She leaned away from Lori, and took it in between her hands.

Softly talking and sipping her drink, she imagined that Lori was listening and smiling inside herself. Her body and mind may have gone into hibernation after all the hard weeks of protecting her gift to them, but Rachel would stay by her side until she awoke. She told her this in many different ways.

"You know how stubborn I can be, well, now that you've given us this amazing gift, it's unlocked in me such new-found resilience and joy that now you're in deep trouble if you think you'll just stay there all quiet."

When her words choked her up again, JT offered her a fresh tissue and leaned to hug her close. "You're amazing, both of you."

She didn't know what time of day it was and it didn't matter. Drinking just enough water to stay hydrated, she made sure she didn't need to take any breaks away from Lori's side. But when JT rubbed her shoulders and asked in low tones if she wanted to go and freshen up, she slowly nodded. She used the washrooms down the corridor and splashed some cold water on her face.

Sitting back, she studied Lori's face and through the ever present lump in her throat she said, "I need you, Lori. Just like I needed you on that day we met at the clinic and over the months when we got so close. You were my angel, and now you've made JT and me a family. But just because you gave us the baby doesn't mean you're done with us, you hear me? I need you because you're the only woman I can truly call my best friend. My true friend. So Dr. Carter's done everything he had to do and now you have to do the rest. You get me? You take a good rest but not too long, because I miss you." She sniffed, blew her nose and took some more breaths. "And you have to see the baby you gave us. You just have to see him. And you know when I'd said that it would be fine if you changed your mind once you see the baby? Well, I take that back, because he's truly our miracle. You knew before I did how it was all going to play out. You're so wise beyond your years."

She massaged Lori's upper arm, down to the swollen fingers and infusing more of her hope into her voice added, "Of course there's also the task of naming the baby, which we'll need your help with. But don't get it wrong, the end decision will be ours, but your input *will* be appreciated."

CHAPTER 54

Only because her mobile phone told Rachel the date and time did she know that it was on the fourth day after Lori had the baby that something finally changed.

A tiny movement under her hand had Rachel instantly awake. She must have dozed off, but she now stared at Lori whose eyes fluttered open and shut.

"Oh my God," Rachel said softly not daring to move, just like she had felt when holding the tiny infant. Oh, the wonderful warmth blossomed inside her as she thought of the baby in its incubator growing stronger with every hour.

Her insides felt all fired up now that she could see her friend slowly waking up from the coma. With the little she knew about it, she hoped that waking up from it within days rather than weeks meant Lori would heal faster without too many side-effects.

A gasp came out of Lori and Rachel blinked away tears while she smiled and scanned her friend's pale face. Her confusion— and was that panic?— seemed to grow as she appeared to work hard on focusing on her surroundings.

Grasping her friend's hand, Rachel slowly explained that she was safe and the baby was healthy and everything would be absolutely fine. Lori's breathing seemed to calm somewhat as if Rachel's trusted words had the right effect.

The nurse came in and started to check the IV drip and moving the tubes around. Then, taking Lori's blood pressure, she nodded and smiled, "Good, let's get Dr. Carter to see you now." Then, raising her bed slightly and gently plumping up the cushions under Lori's head, she asked, "Are you in pain?"

When Lori eventually shook her head slightly the nurse nodded again, "Would you like some water?" When Lori nodded the nurse held a straw to her mouth from a polystyrene cup.

Remembering from her own surgery—which felt like it had happened years ago—she knew how welcome the ice water probably felt to Lori at this moment.

Rachel texted JT, "she's awake" and within minutes he was striding into the room. His first smile was for Rachel as he offloaded a thick sandwich on a plate in her hand and then at Lori's side he said, "You're awake. I'm so glad. You gave us quite a time, you."

Lori's smile was wan but the eyes held a new aliveness that gave Rachel fresh hope.

"Anything for attention, right?" Rachel said. She could have sworn there was a tiny lift on the corners of Lori's lips. But it could have been her wishful thinking.

At the scent of fresh bread and turkey, she salivated, "I'm suddenly very hungry." She grinned. "Are you?"

∼

A small knock at the door introduced a distinguished couple into the room. Just as Lori gasped and her eyes widened, Rachel saw the resemblance of the redheaded man's hazel green eyes.

"Mr. And Mrs. Oliver?" Rachel smiled, shook their hands and quickly introduced JT to them.

"Please, it's Rob and Marilyn." The dark-haired woman who must have been in her early fifties glanced over at the silent Lori and holding her husband's hand smiled, "Thank you for keeping us updated on our daughter's progress. You've been incredible."

Rob nodded and seemed to straighten his tall form as he led Marilyn to Lori's side. "Lori, I'm so glad you're safe now. You brave, brave girl." Tears moistened his eyes as he seemed determined to pull himself together. "Your friends here and Dr. Carter have updated us on everything. And the boys can't wait to come and visit you."

It had only been three days since Lori had gained consciousness and Rachel felt somewhat protective of her friend's emotions and how much she could handle.

But as the slight warm colour brightened Lori's cheeks, she was gratified that she seemed pleased to see her family. Then a small frown furrowed her light brows. Her voice was more of a whisper but Rachel heard her words, "Dad, I hope you're not disappointed but I'm not keeping the baby. I had it for Rachel and James."

Rob nodded and put his hand on his daughter's and now tears came down his face. "I know and I couldn't be more proud of you."

"We're both overwhelmed with your kindness and big heart." Marilyn leaned over and laid a tender kiss on Lori's forehead.

The patent relief and love on her friend's face made Rachel step back a little and as if JT was on the same wavelength, they left the room for the family to reunite and catch up.

∼

Over the next week, Lori insisted on taking less painkillers and took assisted short walks in the corridor and was proud of being able to sit upright in the armchair for a meal.

When Rachel offered to give Lori a hair wash, her friend looked at her as if she had won millions in the lottery. "You'd do that for me?"

"I'd be honoured. You'd do the same for me, wouldn't you?"

"No," Lori smiled and chuckled.

Rachel shook her head, "Your sense of humour's coming back, but you can no longer pretend to be hardhearted with me, I can see right through you."

Carefully helping Lori have her first shower with the help of the medical plastic chair, Rachel heard her friend's big sigh and saw her smile, and couldn't remember if she had the same cleansing, freeing feeling after her hysterectomy over three months ago.

Well, even if she had been depressed, she no longer had any cause to be now.

"I can't tell you how good this feels. I've missed my body and can't wait to get my old body back."

Over the next three weeks, whenever Lori slept or rested, both Rachel and JT spent hours by the baby's incubator, touching him softly, talking with him. Rachel knew she was being a romantic fool but she could have sworn she saw the baby smile and his big ears prick up whenever she touched or talked to him. "Yes, I'm your mummy and I'll spoil you so much and we'll love you so much that you'll never feel alone or scared in this world."

At her request, Rachel was allowed to hold the baby with the nurse's supervision to take him to Lori. But she felt somewhat disoriented as she neared Lori's private room.

"So here's the beautiful little soul all the fuss has been about." Rachel said softly as she brought the tiny wriggling bundle closer to Lori. Obviously, as she couldn't rest the baby on Lori's recovering body, she sat next to her so that her friend could get a better look and touch the baby.

Tension rose within her as she watched the mother and baby connect, as if afraid that the physical bond would change everything to the way nature intended.

"He's perfect." Lori let one finger gently touch the red fist by his face as he tried to open his eyes. "He's absolutely been worth it all... for my two best friends."

When Lori's eyes met hers over the baby and then rested on JT, she smiled. "Now, do you believe me that it was all meant to happen this way?"

Rachel nodded.

"Do either of you have some change or any money?"

JT seemed confused but found a large coin and offered it to Lori. Who took it in her palm and closed her hands over it. "Now this surrogate has been paid for the baby."

Rachel smiled and shook her head, "Again with the drama." But her insides bloomed with such joy that she stood and slowly laid the baby in JT's arms.

"This is the first time I'm holding you, baby." He said and there they were. Father and son, with the tears in the grown man's eyes that were full of happiness and pride. Just like in her dreams.

EPILOGUE

MAY

Rachel glanced around the art exhibition in London's Soho district. It was packed with her sister's friends, regulars from her café and even members of Lori's family. As Rachel held JJ, the six-month-old baby they had named Jordan James, or Jr., she glanced around the noisy but jovial crowds.

JT stood by her like her personal bodyguard, watching his pride and joy, her and their almost chubby growing boy. He grinned as he leaned into her, kissed her temple and held her closer. His eyes gleamed as he watched JJ's big hazel eyes hone in on his second favorite person, his Daddy.

Abby rushed over, glowing with her sense of deserved accomplishment and said, "I still can't believe this is my own solo art show. Can you?"

She tickled JJ under his chin and cooed as Rachel smiled, "Absolutely I can. You're amazing. And Lori said to tell you that she wished she could be here for your special day, but right now Kenya is where she wants to be."

"For now." Abby's eyes sparkled as she glanced up towards the biggest art piece in the centre of the loft-like airy space. "Last month it was India and next month it'll be China... the lucky gallivanter. But at least Rob and Marilyn are here and enjoying the show."

Ever since Lori had been given the complete all clear to travel she had spread her wings and hardly been back home. Having accepted her father's offer to advocate for his company's new all-natural list of products for patients healing from cancer, Lori combined business with her love of travel. Rachel saw on each of their Skype connections how happy and healthy her friend was these days.

"You're very talented, Abby, I'm very proud of my sister-in-law." JT kissed Abby's cheek.

"Thank you, but I feel bad that you bought the piece of JJ. I'd told you it was a gift and I'd give it back to you after the show." She leaned in carefully and sniffed at JJ's reclining head on Rachel's shoulder.

"I insist." JT smiled and his attention seemed to go elsewhere. "That man looks very familiar."

Rachel followed his gaze. "He looks like the man in the painting he's studying."

Abby gasped and her hand shot up to her upper chest and collarbone. "Oh my God, it's Avner."

Rachel felt her sister trembling when she touched her forearm. "Isn't that great?" Her heart blossomed for her. "So go, what are you still doing here?"

"I'm—I'm not ready for any relationships, you know that."

"I don't know that, and maybe he's not here to sweep you off your feet. And if he is, perhaps you can learn to grow together."

Abby looked as scared as on her first ballet recital. But she took in a deep breath and seemed to gather herself. Then she nodded, turned slightly and started making her way towards the tall stranger.

The sleepy JJ started to suck on his thumb nuzzling into her bosom. She smiled at her husband, whom she loved even more now than she had on their wedding day or even last spring. As their son's downy head of thick red hair tickled her chin and jaw she said softly, "I think it's time for this family to go home."

The private look exchanged between them made Rachel feel like the luckiest woman alive.

REVIEW AND GET THE FULL BOOK FREE WITH YOUR LINK

Thank you for reading Nobody's Baby But Mine
If you enjoyed it, please take an extra two minutes to review it now on the last page of this ebook. Please email me the link of your review and I will send you the full book free a few days after it's published.

Thank you so much in advance!

End of 2018 you can also read HEALING LOVE, Abby's poignant story or healing, learning to love herself and letting love into her life.

In the meantime discover **more about the author or stories by Gloria Silk now.**

Subscribe to Gloria Silk's newsletter now
Or follow Gloria Silk on **Facebook**

BOOK CLUB QUESTIONS

1. How did you feel about the beginning of the novel? Did it grab your attention or did you have to read more to get into the story?
2. Which parts stood out for you, and why?
3. Which characters made you suspicious or unsure about their integrity, and why? Did this change throughout the story?
4. How credible were the characters; Rachel, James, Abby and Lauren? Who did you find annoying/frustrating and why?
5. Which characters did you sympathize with and why? Did this change through the novel?
6. Who did you feel had the biggest emotional growth, and why?
7. Which plot points do you feel were well depicted, and which aspects do you feel were too unrealistic, and why?
8. Did you notice any themes throughout the book?
9. If Rachel Windsor had chosen Brandon Ross ten years ago or even this time around, how do you think the story may have played out?
10. What would you have liked the author to describe in more detail?
11. Which characters would you have liked to get to know better, deeper, and why?
12. How did you feel about the pacing and the unfolding of the story? Were there any slow parts and any that were glossed over?
13. Was the ending to your liking, and why?

14. If it was not satisfying what would you have liked the author to have done differently?
15. How did this book affect your opinions about any subjects discussed in the novel? What are the most touching and surprising aspects, and why?
16. If you imagine this novel made into a movie, would you still like it set in London or elsewhere?
17. And which actors would you imagine to play the main characters' roles, and why?

GLORIA SILK'S BOOKS

Do you believe in love at first sight?

First love has never been more intense, heartbreaking, and oh so worth it!

Shy artist Lia cannot resist gorgeous genius, Devraj. One rain soaked kiss changes the landscape of both their lives forever as sparks fly and their families and friends try to break them apart. Will Lia's loyalty to her cultural ties force her to forsake her forbidden love or can she stand up for her first and only love and face their uncharted future head on?

Amazon ASIN: B00N7VTCE4 iBooks Nook KOBO Google Play Google Books

Debut novel, First and Only Destiny

"Beautifully written love story with a perfect happy ever after. The prose in this book is extraordinary, the emotions heart-breaking and the author leaves you hanging on the edge right to the end of the story..." **Elizabeth Lennox**, Author of the Thorpe Brothers series

WHAT CAME NEXT?

In the end of *First and Only Destiny* Lia and Devraj finally got their well-deserved Happily Ever After!

BUT! Then I wondered what if instead of living the rest of their lives together in bliss they were torn apart?

So I wrote **Second Destiny** where almost twenty years later Lia is a mother of two and married. On the day Lia realizes she cannot stay in her loveless marriage to the 'right' Jewish man chosen by her grandparents decades earlier, Devraj is at her door trying to protect his nephew and Lia's 18 year-old daughter from repeating their own star-crossed love affair?

Well, read SECOND DESTINY now! BUY SECOND DESTINY

Years ago, the older generation broke Lia and Devraj apart. Now, the younger generation reunites them.

Lia's world turns upside down again when minutes after she demands a divorce from her cheating husband, Devraj is at her door. Will Lia again choose duty over the desires of her heart?

BUY NOW: Amazon ASIN: B00N7YI3CI
iBooks Nook Kobo Google Play Google Books

From Geek To Greek Billionaire is the international stand-alone bestseller about a second chance at romance between a shy, gorgeous geek billionaire Alexander, who is back in Wrightsville Beach on a love mission, and interior designer Olivia who is keeping secrets she cannot share with him.

Amazon ASIN: B077TH57PC

iBooks Nook Kobo Google Play Google Books

End 2018: Healing Love - After beautiful young artist's craving for love endangers her restaurant business and her life she resolves to get help. How can she turn her life around and find everlasting love if her nightmares keep recurring?

FOR MORE ABOUT GLORIA SILK AND HER BOOKS VISIT WWW.GLORIASILK.COM

BECOME ARC REVIEWER = MORE GREAT BOOKS FOR FREE!

Enjoyed this book? Please take a couple of minutes to **review it**.

Love free ARCs (advance reading copies) then please join GS Review Team for free: **SUBSCRIBE TO GLORIA SILK'S NEWSLETTER NOW.**
Follow Gloria Silk on **FACEBOOK**
DISCOVER MORE ABOUT GLORIA SILK AND HER NOVELS NOW

WHY SHOULD YOU JOIN THE ARC TEAM?

All any author wants is to know that her readers are loving and enjoying her stories.

The best way is always word of mouth, so go ahead and tell your friends about your favorite books and consider reviewing them.

As a member of the **Gloria Silk Review Team** read your chosen free books from me and leave an honest review once you've **actually** read it, (on your chosen book seller's platform). Your review can be as short or as long as you have time for. This will help other readers enjoy my books too. **Thank you, dear reader!**

To join the **Gloria Silk Review Team** and receive Advance Reading Copies and more free goodies please email: **CONTACT@GLORIASILK.COM** - and add in the subject: "Joining the Gloria Silk ARC Team" or *SUBSCRIBE NOW*.

SUBSCRIBE TO GLORIA SILK'S (MONTHLY) NEWSLETTER NOW. AND FOLLOW HER ON FACEBOOK

For more about Gloria Silk and her books visit www.GloriaSilk.com

ABOUT GLORIA SILK

Ever since Gloria Silk was little her passion was creating and sharing her romantic stories with others. She always loved reading contemporary and historical novels that grasped her imagination. Gloria now writes intense, sensuous love stories with happy endings.

In addition to writing romance and women's fiction, she enjoys writing intercultural romances and about family bonds. What can be more important in life than love and family?

Born in Russia, Gloria Silk has visited and lived in amazing, exotic places, including some in Europe and the Mediterranean. Her favourite in the world, by far is Hawaii.

Being a writer gives her the privilege to explore, travel, and meet wonderful, new and exciting—and sometimes eccentric—people. Her background in English literature, writing, and psychology all help her create unique characters for her stories. Especially her charismatic heroes and feisty heroines who find themselves in sticky situations with each other, their families, and their cultures. There is nothing more satisfying than knowing readers love her warm heroines and the gorgeous enigmatic heroes, as she falls in love with them too.

When she is not painting in various media or watching

romantic movies, or cooking up a storm for her family and friends, she hangs out with her writing friends and other creatives.

Although she was brought up in England, she now lives—and writes—in the Toronto suburbs in Ontario, Canada, with her husband and daughter.

Partial proceeds of all Gloria Silk's book sales are donated towards cancer research.

For More Information visit
www.GloriaSilk.com
contact@gloriasilk.com

www.ingramcontent.com/pod-product-compliance
Lightning Source LLC
Chambersburg PA
CBHW070538010526
44118CB00012B/1167